Laura Gay: a novel.

Laura Gay

The BiblioLife Network

This project was made possible in part by the BiblioLife Network (BLN), a project aimed at addressing some of the huge challenges facing book preservationists around the world. The BLN includes libraries, library networks, archives, subject matter experts, online communities and library service providers. We believe every book ever published should be available as a high-quality print reproduction; printed on- demand anywhere in the world. This insures the ongoing accessibility of the content and helps generate sustainable revenue for the libraries and organizations that work to preserve these important materials.

The following book is in the "public domain" and represents an authentic reproduction of the text as printed by the original publisher. While we have attempted to accurately maintain the integrity of the original work, there are sometimes problems with the original book or micro-film from which the books were digitized. This can result in minor errors in reproduction. Possible imperfections include missing and blurred pages, poor pictures, markings and other reproduction issues beyond our control. Because this work is culturally important, we have made it available as part of our commitment to protecting, preserving, and promoting the world's literature.

GUIDE TO FOLD-OUTS, MAPS and OVERSIZED IMAGES

In an online database, page images do not need to conform to the size restrictions found in a printed book. When converting these images back into a printed bound book, the page sizes are standardized in ways that maintain the detail of the original. For large images, such as fold-out maps, the original page image is split into two or more pages.

Guidelines used to determine the split of oversize pages:

• Some images are split vertically; large images require vertical and horizontal splits.
• For horizontal splits, the content is split left to right.
• For vertical splits, the content is split from top to bottom.
• For both vertical and horizontal splits, the image is processed from top left to bottom right.

12630.c.8.

LAURA GAY.

A NOVEL.

IN TWO VOLUMES.
VOL. II.

LONDON:
HURST AND BLACKETT, PUBLISHERS,
SUCCESSORS TO HENRY COLBURN,
13, GREAT MARLBOROUGH STREET.
1856.

LONDON:
Printed by Schulze and Co., 13, Poland Street.

LAURA GAY.

———◆———

CHAPTER I.

NEARLY four months have now elapsed since we left Laura to pursue her melancholy reflections on the change that had come o'er the spirit of her dream, and the feelings of her lover. She was then on the point of returning to North Wales.

During the journey thither, she debated with herself whether she should impart to her aunt all that had passed at the Flower Show. It would certainly be a very great

relief to unbosom herself to so affectionate
and sympathizing a relative; but then, she
knew that the recital of her sorrows would
deeply grieve her aunt, who would probably
blame herself for having approved and
encouraged Laura's intimacy with Charles
Thornton. Mrs. Owen's health, too, was
now so delicate, that any shock to her
spirits was much to be feared. Laura
resolved, therefore, to avoid all mention
of Thornton; at least, until she had recovered a greater composure in thinking
of him, and more self-command in naming
him.

She hoped that early acquired habits of
study would now stand her in good stead,
and that by dint of self-discipline she might
regain a portion of her cheerfulness and interest in life; little foreseeing, poor girl,
the fresh trials in store for her.

The carriage met her at the station,
and had she been less pre-occupied, she

would have perceived, at once, that Williams had painful intelligence to communicate.

Laura's maid, whose volubility exceeded that of the worthy butler, told him, in alighting, how ill and hysterical her mistress had been in town.

This increased his embarrassment; and after a short parley, he reopened the carriage door, and putting in a small basket, asked if Miss Gay would not stop at Dr. Evans's in their way through the small market-town of Glynsbryun.

" Surely, my dear aunt is not ill !" said she, trembling with alarm.

" Yes, Miss, we're afraid as Missus is very ill, and don't think Mr. Jones understands the case."

" Oh !" groaned Laura, with anguish, to think she had been absent at such a crisis, "yes, by all means stop at Dr. Evans's, and tell James not to mind the horses at all, but to go as fast as possible."

Laura was overwhelmed with apprehension and grief, and so ill prepared by what she had just gone through, to bear up against further afflictions, that she fancied herself about to give way, and to become altogether helpless. Her limbs trembled, her head was giddy, her very voice seemed likely to forsake her; and she had the greatest difficulty to summon up energy sufficient to speak to Dr. Evans, when they reached his door.

It was immediately agreed that he should accompany her home—an arrangement he might well have regretted, had he not been a good-natured and phlegmatic physician; for Laura, in her excitement, and strongly oppressed with the urgency of the case, determined to lose no time, and without precisely knowing the nature of her aunt's present illness, entered so fully

into all the particulars of Mrs. Owen's
constitution, and all the morbid symptoms
she had ever known her manifest, that
had Dr. Evans been listening to her conversation, he might have formed a very
incorrect notion of the malady he was expected to prescribe for. As they approached
the house, he said, with professional authority and earnestness;

"Now, Miss Gay, you must wipe away
all traces of those tears, or they may do
your aunt more harm than they can do you
good."

She managed to obey; and they proceeded
together, Laura on the tiptoe of anxiety,
to Mrs. Owen's bed-side. She was lying
in a restless doze; her breathing was
quick and difficult, her hands and face
were burning hot; and Mrs. Slater, who
was sitting in the room, said she thought
her mistress had wandered a little before
she had fallen asleep.

Laura saw Dr. Evans shake his head,
as he felt Mrs. Owen's pulse, and listened
to her breathing. He retired with Laura
into the dressing-room, and beckoned Mrs.
Slater to follow.

"When was your mistress taken ill?"

"Why, sir, some three or four days ago,
Missus complained, over-night, of shivers,
and took some white wine whey. She
seemed rather weakish the next morning;
but then she had a very good colour, and
the day was sultry, and nobody thought
nothing of it."

"And when did you first become
alarmed?"

"Why, sir, the night before last Mrs.
Owen had the shivers again very bad; and
her breathing got troublesome, and she had
a bad pain in her side, and we put
mustard plasters on, and yesterday morning
we sent for Mr. Jones, and he put on
leeches."

"Jones? humph! Are you sure he did not bleed?"

"No, sir; we should have sent for you, but Missus thought it better to wait for Miss Gay to come home, before we decided to do so. You see, sir, Missus is very tender-hearted, and does not like to offend people; and she thought, perhaps, Mr. Jones might be hurt; besides, as I said before, Missus leaves everything for Miss Gay to decide."

Poor Laura sighed bitterly. How willingly, at that moment, she would have sacrificed all the influence her intelligence gave her, to have been relieved of the load of responsibility it entailed.

"What can you do?" said she.

"We must send for Jones immediately. He must make up the prescription I am about to write, and bring a blister and the necessary dressings. In the mean time, we must bleed. I will stay an hour or two with you, and to-morrow I will come again, and if you think proper, I will bring a nurse to sit up at night with your aunt, for she will require the greatest attention and care for many weeks, if we are fortunate in our remedies, as I trust we may be," said he, proceeding with a candle to Mrs. Owen's bedside. She was scarcely conscious when he began to bleed her, and although he shook his head very ominously, as the blood flowed, yet Laura gathered hope, as she observed the anxious expression of her aunt's features give way, and the difficulty of breathing abate.

The attack was one of pleurisy. Had bleeding been resorted to, at the outset, it might have been successful; but an abscess had formed in the lungs, which Dr. Evans said it might be just possible to disperse by the use of powerful depletives.

Mrs. Owen's illness assumed a lingering character, and some weeks before it terminated fatally, Laura had relinquished every hope of any other result. Notwithstanding the nature of the disease, the restlessness it occasioned never became impatience, unless we may call the sufferer's longing for death, by that name.

What regretful memories—what a chilling prospect of loneliness tortured the poor watcher's heart during those dreary days of ebbing life; yet, for the dear invalid's sake, her niece maintained an outward composure, ill-bespeaking the anguish she endured.

One day, especially, of that long illness, was graven for ever upon Laura's memory. It was her twenty-first birth-day. She had risen almost at day-break to attend upon her aunt; the morning was sultry: towards noon, Dr. Evans came, and both he and her aunt begged her to go to bed, and try to get a little sleep. She obeyed their wishes, but derived no refreshment from her slumbers. At one moment, she stood, in her dream, beside the bed of her dying father. He held Thornton by the hand, and blessing him, bade him protect her through life; but Thornton looked stern and estranged, and seemed to say the engagement was too onerous. She thought she made signs, that he should only let her father suppose he would do it, and she would cancel his promise afterwards. Then Mrs. Redford, Mrs. Owen, and Lady Cecilia surrounded her; she sought to weep, but pride and shame forbad it, and she started up to shake off sleep, and drown sorrow in tears.

Fearing lest her aunt should ask for her before she had time to recover herself, she went out, and seated herself under a magnificent lime tree in front of the house. It grew tall and erect, and its drooping branches touched the lawn, forming, at this time, a most verdant, fragrant, and musical tent, for it was early in August, and the season being late, the tree was still in full flower, and its branches alive with myriads of insects, sucking in honey and happiness.

Their hum, and the recollection of many calm and happy hours, spent with her father and her brother beneath that leafy canopy, came over her and soothed her. She remembered the many conversations, in which her father had been the chief speaker, and the topic, the responsibilities that might probably commence for her on that twenty-first birth-day.

With pain, too, she recalled the dreams she had indulged in at Rome, of the joy with which, about this time, she should welcome another, whom, in the delusion of passion, she had endowed with all the virtues of her father, to share her wealth and her responsibilities, and to claim her wifely devotion. Even now, unworthy as she deemed him in comparison, her inconstant lover still lived in her affections, and far too constantly in her thoughts. How exquisitely painful was the contrast between *his* cold indifference, *his* continued silence, and the kind inquiries which came almost daily [from young Mr. and Mrs. Owen at the Hall, from neighbours and friends in Yorkshire, from friends like Lord Huntley at a distance; whilst *he* who had known them both, her aunt and herself so well, though so recently, seemed to feel no further interest in them.

Great was the bitterness of such meditations, nor was it in any degree alleviated on her return to the sick room of her aunt, who asked where she had been, and tenderly wishing her many happy returns of the day; alluded with satisfaction to the affluence in which she would be left, and the excellent man who would shortly become her acknowledged protector.

"I am very glad, my darling, now, that I acquiesced in that suggestion of yours at

Rome, concerning the loan to Charles Thornton. You will tell him, when I am gone, how glad I was to do so, and then he will know that I liked him, and you will be able to talk to him about me, as you sit together under the lime tree,.

A day or two previous to her death, Mrs. Owen, calling Laura to her bedside, inquired if she thought Charles Thornton would be likely to come to see her before her departure.

"No, dearest aunt, I fear it is impossible," replied Laura with painful confusion.

The sad solemn hour of separation, at last, drew nigh. Laura had been reading some of those sure and touching promises which bring the Saviour of men to comfort us in our mortal extremity: she was kneeling behind the bed curtain, breathing a confused prayer, that the pains and struggles of death, might be mitigated to her aunt, and that she,

herself, might be supported under the
affliction of losing one so endeared to her,
when she heard her name feebly uttered.
Laura rose, and stood by the bedside.

"Laura," said her aunt, with a decision
strangely differing from her former self;
"I am going whither you must wish to
come; but you have a stewardship, my
child, to fufil. Tell Charles Thornton I said
so. Give him my blessing, as he has often
had my prayers; tell him he has your
father's blessing, too; tell him there is
but one sure and stable prop to
human virtue—but one road to a happy
end; and he must tread that road with
you."

Laura's heart could no longer contain
its grief; she was convulsed with
sobs.

"Nay, nay, my dear child," continued
her aunt, with difficulty, "do not sorrow
as one without hope. You have no right

to do so; you are surrounded with all that can promote the happiness and usefulness of life; you must learn to bear its trials bravely, and to prove your faith by your resignation.

"Recollect your dear father: his bereavement exceeded yours.

"I have one little request to make," she added; " do not forget my sister-in-law, Miss Owen. Let her pay her annual visit here, every autumn. This is but a small enjoyment to secure to my dear husband's sister. I made a little note, explaining my wishes respecting her, some time ago. You will find it among my papers. I am sure that both Mr. Thornton and you will attend to it."

Laura promised to do so; and another long pause ensued, followed by a slight convulsion, during which Laura felt her hand clasped—a look of ineffable satis-

faction—and the spirit departed, as the
lips murmured forth the words of the
Psalmist :

" Praise the Lord ! oh, my soul !"

With fond affection, Laura pressed the
dying hand, and gently closed the
peaceful eyes.   Then, at last, came the
full burst of her own woe ; and in this
last blow, the whole burden of her former
sorrows descended upon her.   Her aunt,
it is true, had not been of much importance to her, either as an adviser or
a protectress : still, she had always been
an affectionate and devoted friend, whose
sympathy and love had stood between
the orphan and the world ; and many
were the recollections and the consolations
the two had shared as they conversed
together of the dear departed ones.

Poor Laura had never felt so desolate,
or so devoid of energy ; and, when the
last sad funeral rites were over, and her

aunt's body reposed in the churchyard beside her uncle's and her brother's, she felt as though the happiness, and the value of life had passed away, and nothing but an aching void remained.

Kind messages, and kind letters came pouring in from the friends who had loved and valued Laura or her aunt; but serviceable as such condolences sometimes are to divert the mind from the poignancy of its grief, in this instance, they did but remind Laura that she had not one friend left in the world to whom she could open her whole heart; so she answered them all kindly or politely, as the case demanded, and laid them by, with a hopeless sigh, near those she had received on the occasion of her brother's and her father's death.

Mr. Jenkins came down from town, to remind her that she was the sole heiress of her aunt's property, and to offer her any assistance she might require in its management.

When he saw Miss Gay's dejected and delicate appearance, he urged her most earnestly and kindly, to try a complete change of scene and air. Mrs. Jenkins was staying at Folkestone, where she had taken a house for the months of September and October. She had plenty of spare room, having but one little daughter, and her governess staying with her. Miss Gay should have her own apartment, and just as much of Mrs. Jenkins' society as she found she could bear.

Mr. Jenkins's offer was supported by the strong recommendations of good Mistress Slater and of Mr. Williams, the butler; both of whom, feeling that a change would be beneficial to their own health, after so much anxiety and distress, were quite certain that it was absolutely necessary for their young mistress. Laura's listlessness was such, that she was easily led to accept the invitation; and the journey to Folkestone, was fixed for the following week, on Mrs. Slater's assertion, that it would be impossible to complete their mourning suits, and to make the necessary arrangements for leaving home within a shorter period.

Mr. Jenkins returned to town, and ran down to Folkestone for a day, to inform his wife of the honour he had procured her.

Mrs. Jenkins was a bustling, sensible, good-natured woman of the world, that is, of the society to which she belonged. She had a hearty appetite, hearty health, a hearty affection for Mr. Jenkins and her children, and a hearty love of society with all its formal and material adjuncts; and she was never insensible to anything which might promote her husband's business connections, or increase her own importance. Loking forward, therefore, with pleasure to Miss Gay's visit, she made every possible preparation to secure the comfort and freedom of her guest. She insisted, in particular, with Miss Flora and the governess, that no remarks were to be made, not even by looks, on her mourning dress, or the sadness of her manner; and that Flora was not to importune her with attentions. She likewise gave orders to her servants that Miss Gay's maid should always be asked, whether her mistress would take her meals alone, or with the family.

It so happened, that just about the time that Laura reached Folkestone, Mrs. Redford came there too, with her mother, to whose care Redford had consigned his wife; he, himself, having accepted an invitation to shoot in Scotland, and his return being uncertain. Mrs. Redford had chosen the Hotel at Folkestone, to escape trouble, and in the hope of being enlivened by the traffic of tourists perpetually passing through it. Indeed, so little had she found in her life of luxury to call forth the activity of heart or head, that without society, she felt as she said *ennuyée jusqu'à se pendre.*

In society vanity was her ruling passion, and she seemed to possess abundant means for its gratification. Handsomer than before her marriage, at liberty, as only married women are, to please, and rich enough to bestow on her person those auxiliary charms created by the *couturière* and the *modiste,* a more stylish looking belle could hardly be met with.

The stream of travellers was, however, unpropitious to Mrs. Redford's amusement, for few appeared at Folkestone whom she knew, or chose to recognize, and she and her mother were meditating a removal to St. Leonard's or Brighton, when she discovered that Miss Gay was staying at

Folkestone with Mrs. Jenkins. How this should influence her determination to remain, it is not difficult to explain. She was prompted by curiosity and vanity. She longed to see whether Laura's charms had fared so well as her own. Would they not be spoiled by cold celibacy and watching, by sorrow and disappointment, such as *she* could more easily imagine than experience?

Moreover, she supposed that Miss Gay might have come thither in the hope of renewing her intimacy with Charles Thornton; and she thought it not impossible that Mr. Jenkins, whom she ascertained to be Miss Gay's solicitor, might be employed to arrange a meeting, to bring about a reconciliation, and to divulge the source of the loan. The exposure with which this threatened her, her *penchant* for Thornton, and her dislike of Miss Gay, all spurred her on to unwonted efforts of activity, in order to prevent such a rencontre. For

LAURA GAY.23

this purpose, she resolved to establish a communication, direct or indirect, betwixt herself and Miss Gay.

She made numerous inquiries of her servants, interspersed with some expressions of compassion, respecting Miss Gay, and soon learnt from her maid, that she was staying for change of air with Mrs. Jenkins, whose acquaintance she had only just made, that she kept herself very much to herself, and indulged in very low spirits. They also whispered that she was very proud, on account of her great fortune, the amount of which Mrs. Redford's maid had heard, and could tell exactly. It was also reported to Mrs. Redford that Miss Gay was attended by her old maid and man servant, who shared among Mrs. Jenkins' servants, their mistress's reputation for pride and exclusiveness. Williams, especially, was an object of animadversion, because he used words, and talked on subjects which his auditors did not understand, taking but little notice of them, and no interest in their gossip and criticism of their betters. So Mrs. Jenkins' kitchen coterie gave him credit for a hypocritical profession of piety and attachment to his young mistress, and made a set at his gravity, thus becoming as coteries frequently do, the ready instruments, in the hands of malice, for torturing innocence and virtue.

Mrs. Redford tasked her ingenuity to the utmost, to devise a successful scheme of operations. From infancy, she had been taught to believe that a knowledge of the foibles and the vices of mankind gives a vantage ground to those who are clever in its application. Her mother was almost intuitively possessed of this science; and though Mrs. Redford inherited it in a minor degree, still her six months' experience of married life had sharpened both perceptively and inventively her knowledge of evil. She took her maid to walk with her on the beach; condescendingly encouraging the girl to prattle for her amusement, and agreeing with her that Mr. Williams had an eye to the loaves and fishes. "But," added she, carelessly "if a certain person whom I know, could only be bribed by Miss Gay to marry her, Williams, no doubt, would soon change his methodistic professions."

"La!" said the girl, "there's many-a-one would have such a pretty lady as Miss Gay, and be glad, without a bribe beforehand, I should think, ma'am."

"So should I," replied Mrs. Redford, in the same careless tone. "I should think Miss Gay's fortune would secure her scores of offers; and therefore I am surprised that she should have set her heart on a person who does not care for her."

"Dear me! has she, ma'am?—what a pity! Well to be sure, what a queer

world this is! Only think of such a rich
young lady bribing any one to marry her.
That's more than I'd do."

"It is very silly to make advances to
men; they only despise you for it; and
I pity Miss Gay, poor thing! for I have
been told she was desperately in love with
him."

"Poor young lady! it's a great pity
nobody tells her the truth," said the maid,
with the virtuous intention of doing her
petit possible towards enlightening Miss
Gay on the subject; for she was of the
Bloomer caste, and had a grudge against
obdurate men, founded on personal experience, which impelled her to wish them
the scornful neglect of the fair.

After a pause, during which Mrs. Redford
appeared to be reflecting, she added; " of
course, I don't wish you to go about spreading
false reports; in fact, I don't know *for
certain* that Miss Gay has bribed any one;

I only *suspect* it, from what I have heard him say, to the disparagement of women who do such things."

"Well, really how deceitful men are! Dear me, ma'am, I should think I have something else to do than to be talking about everywhere. Only to think of his boasting of it—well to be sure, dear me, wonders never cease!"

The seeds of scandal were sown in a fruitful soil; and Mrs. Redford's insinuations were soon used to torment the faithful and taciturn Mr. Williams. He stoutly denied the whole story, asserting it to be impossible, since Miss Gay had only just become possessed of her fortune; and he challenged his persecutors to name their authority, and the person whom Miss Gay was said to have courted and bribed. His tormentors declared they had his name on the best authority, but did not choose to be bullied into telling it. Mrs. Slater shared

Mr. Williams's indignation, and his certainty that the story was false. Under these circumstances, she related it to her young mistress, almost hoping to induce her to seek out its originators, and .to hold them up to exposure.

Laura, however, seemed only shocked and distressed by it, and talked of leaving Folkestone very shortly. She had already seen Mrs. Redford at a distance, and had carefully avoided every chance of meeting her; nor could she help believing that Thornton, having divined the lender, had mentioned the loan, and under the fascination of an illicit attachment, had given utterance to ungenerous sentiments quite unworthy the character with which her fond attachment had invested him. These circumstances roused her to shake off the lethargy of grief, perhaps more effectually than the voice of friendly counsel could have done.

Painful experience had taught her that, if in health and prosperity, we only seek our own gratification, disappointment, and vexation of spirit will ensue. She strove, therefore, to regard both, as means entrusted to her for a higher purpose.

Hitherto, she had relinquished, more in sorrow than in anger, her hopes of happiness and union with Charles Thornton. Irritation against him, and shame to think how misplaced her affections and generosity had been, now coloured her disappointment ; for, with all her amiability, Laura was a spirited girl ; and her standard of masculine virtue was a high one. Ceasing, therefore, to invoke the return of her lover's affections, she even resolved, in her own mind, that, should he tire of his present *penchant*, and seek a renewal of her love, duty would compel her to refuse it with indignation.

To duty alone she would con-
secrate herself with just such fervour
as carried the wounded spirits of old
into the cloister and the hermit's
cell. As yet, perchance, the tones of
the shepherd's voice had not pene-
trated her heart; and she might not
know that he spoke of duty—the offspring
of law and of life, of free-will and fate
—when he said:

" Come unto me all ye that are weary
and heavy laden, and I will give you rest.
Take my yoke upon you, and learn of me;
for I am meek and lowly in heart; and ye
shall find rest unto your souls. For my yoke
is easy, and my burthen light.

However, duty, whether understood in
a natural or a non-natural sense, requires
a plan and a scene. Henceforth, the
former should engross the whole of her
thoughts; and to the latter she would hie
with all decent speed.

Thanking Mrs. Jenkins at dinner, that day, for her very considerate hospitality, she informed her, that in a day or two she must conclude her visit. Mrs. Jenkins thought it a great pity that Miss Gay should leave at the very time, when she appeared to be deriving the greatest benefit from the sea air.

Laura's cordiality and Mrs. Jenkins' friendship increased as the hour of departure drew near. Even Miss Flora, and the governess, were mollified, and the whole household began to accuse Mrs. Redford's maid of being a mischief-making gossip.

The day previous to her return home, Laura had sallied forth to a distant part of the cliff, to enjoy a last and solitary gaze over the watery expanse, and to imbibe a milder breeze than usually comes across the sea in the early part of October. There was a sparkling rythmical dance going on

among the waves, while a broad and mellow
sunlight cast itself over the cliff, and on
the Downs, seeming to proclaim the geniality
of nature, and her power to bestow pleasures of a serene and durable kind, quite
independent of passion and human intercourse.

Laura had not sat there long, before she
perceived a lady, a boy, and a tall young
girl approaching her. There was something in the elasticity of their movements,
and in the quiet gaiety of their dress, that
harmonized well with the cheerful tone of
the scene, and made them agreeable figures
in the landscape.

As such, she was regarding them, when
suddenly she perceived the trio to be
no other than Lady Cecilia Mowbray, and
her two children. Their surprise equalled
her own, and the kindest greetings passed
between them.

"When did you come here?" asked Laura.

" The evening before last."

" How long shall you stay ?"

" Only a day or two. We came from Ryde, where we have been spending a few weeks to recruit Eustace after the measles; and we have come here to meet Mr. Mowbray on his return from the continent; but how long have you been here, and where are you staying ?"

" I have been here, almost ever since my poor aunt's death, and I am staying with Mrs. Jenkins, the wife of my solicitor, who kindly offered to receive me, for change of air and scene. To-morrow, I return home."

Lady Cecilia repressed a sigh, for Laura was sadly changed in appearance; and she recollected that, notwithstanding her wealth, she was an orphan, and, probably, rather friendless in the world.

" Go my dears," said her ladyship to the young people; " amuse yourselves as you like, only keep in sight of us."

Laura buried her face in her handkerchief and wept: for the young brother and sister's companionship recalled vividly, the many joyous days now gone for ever, when she too rejoiced in the love of her brother, her father, and her aunt, and had known and cared for no other.

"Don't weep, dear," said Lady Cecilia, soothingly, as she seated herself by Laura's side, partly guessing the associations which roused her grief, "but let us talk of your present plans, and try to regard them in a cheerful light."

"I was revolving them in my mind when you came up."

"Well, in the first place, I hope you will not live alone."

"I don't know. Perhaps you are aware that my dear aunt left a sister-in-law—Miss Owen, who usually spent every October with her. I have invited her to spend this month with me, so that, at present, I am provided with a companion."

"Ah, yes! I think I remember once meeting her mother, Lady Helen Owen. I fear you will find her rather a gloomy and narrow-minded companion just now. It strikes me, she is one of the unco-gude, and, therefore, unlikely to prove either very interesting or very considerate. Such persons are too deeply engrossed in their own salvation and righteousness, to interest themselves in other people's feelings."

"I am bound to entertain her, out of regard to my aunt's memory," replied Laura, "besides, my dear father always used to say that our first social duties are those we owe to relatives, connections and neighbours; and I think he was right—one may go farther and fare worse—we are acquainted with *their* faults, and run no risk, therefore, of being suddenly distressed or shocked by them."

"When Miss Owen leaves you, what shall you do?"

"As regards a companion, I cannot tell yet. I shall have time before then to consider, and determine upon some one. I intend to reside chiefly at Sexhurst in Yorkshire, because amid the large manufacturing population in that neighbourhood, I expect to find more employment for my time and thoughts than at Llanbeddwr, where the population is very sparse, very Welsh, and already provided with benefactors at the Hall and the parsonage."

"Oh, yes! I have heard that Mr. and Mrs. Owen are very agreeable young people. She is a sister of Lord Huntley's—is she not?"

"Yes," said Laura, "I believe they are agreeable. She is pretty, and has the reputation of being a good artist, and a good horsewoman; but they did not come to the Hall immediately on their marriage : they spent nearly two years abroad, and returned about the time of my brother's death ; since then, my own trials, and absence from the Dell have prevented my seeing enough of them to know what sort of people they really are."

" And the parson—what sort of a man is he ?"

" Both he and his wife are excellent people, simple in piety, in tastes, in habits ; industrious and sensible. Beyond these two families, there are two or three others of country gentry, and country clergy, who are quite undistinguishable from the same class of persons any where else."

" Well, and who are your neighbours at Sexhurst ?"

" People whom *you* would call nobody—yet they are very numerous ; with few exceptions their speech betrayeth them ; they have not the sort of cultivation you would recognize. On the contrary, they have the spirit of trade *très prononcé*. Still they are capable and interesting people, possessing, in common with ourselves, the natural frailties and virtues, which, after all, if you penetrate a very superficial crust, make all classes of human beings very much resemble each other."

"Take care, my dear Laura," said her ladyship, smiling, "how you settle down amongst them. There, you will have no stimulus to self-improvement. You will be a Queen amongst them, and you will find it more easy to contract their inferiority, than to impart your own superiority."

"I shall keep a strict guard over myself. I know that vulgarity and selfishness are the inevitable consequences of isolated superiority, either of talent or of station, and of a life of total seclusion. So, by way of a mutual benefit, I shall propose that Mr. Mowbray, yourself, and your children, should visit me occasionally at Sexhurst, to keep me up to what the *beau monde* calls 'polite society,' and in return I think I can show you, that a very worthy and agreeable society may be formed altogether without its pale."

"Thank you, and depend upon our accepting your invitation for your own sake, if not for that of the introduction to the society of the neighbourhood."

"I have an excellent library also at Sexhurst," continued Laura, "very carefully selected by my father and myself, where Mr. Mowbray may consult political and statistical authorities to his heart's content."

"Do you intend to study much yourself?"

"Yes, I intend to divide my day, and to give, at least, three hours every morning, to the same sort of study and reading I have hitherto pursued; by this means, I hope to preserve both manners and mind, and to keep alive those aspirations after virtue and wisdom, that give a permanent object and charm to life."

There was a pause, which Lady Cecilia broke by saying:

"I think Mr. Mowbray will arrive here by the afternoon boat, together with Mr. Thornton, who has been his companion throughout the tour."

Laura started, and with difficulty concealed her agitation.

"I presume you do not wish to meet the latter, and, therefore, I will not press you to dine with us at the hotel; for you know, I cannot tell what invitation Mr. Mowbray may have given."

"Thank you," said Laura, "I could hardly have left Mrs. Jenkins to dine out to-day, especially as I leave her altogether to-morrow."

Lady Cecilia looked at her watch, and they rose to seek the young people, who had seated themselves to sketch at some distance on the cliff.

She remarked as they went along, to her

now silent companion, that Charles Thornton
was a strange compound of good and ill;
that her husband had a great regard for
him, and a great respect for his judgment
and high principle, and that it was very
unwillingly he brought himself to believe
in the connection subsisting between Mrs.
Redford and his young friend, and," added
her ladyship, "like most men, he lays the
chief blame on the seductive powers of the
lady, who, by the bye, I was greatly surprised to find staying without her husband
at the hotel here, in the full force of
fashion and beauty, probably awaiting the
arrival of Mr. Thornton."

Laura sighed, and nodded assent to the
cause assigned for Mrs. Redford's visit to
Folkestone.

"Do you know, Laura," added her ladyship, "my husband's account of Mr. Thornton had almost induced me to blame myself
for what I told you in the spring, and I had

begun to think that the report of his *liaison* with Mrs. Redford was a scandal, to which his inexperience of the conventionalities of society had exposed him; but now I absolve myself of an uncharitable credulity, for the fact of Mrs. Redford's being here just now, seems conclusive evidence against him."

The two ladies rejoined the children, who were very glad to renew their acquaintance with Miss Gay, and were much pleased to hear that they were to spend some time at Sexhurst in the winter. Having accompanied her to Mrs. Jenkins's house, they bade her adieu—*au revoir.*

During lunch, Mrs. Jenkins made endless inquiries about Lady Cecilia Mowbray and her family. Laura's thoughts were abstracted, and her answers did not afford much information.

Meanwhile, the Boulogne boat had landed its load of passengers. Lady Cecilia and

her children were on the quay to welcome
Mr. Mowbray, who was surprised and delighted to see them, and placing his wife's
arm affectionately within his own, proceeded
to the hotel. Mr. Thornton and the two
children followed, and they exclaimed almost
together :

"Guess, Mr. Thornton, whom we met
on the cliff here this morning."

"I fear I cannot; was it any one, I
know ?"

"Of course it was," said Susan.

"Was it Mrs. Redford ?"

"No, though Mrs. Redford *is* here," said
Susan.

"Then I cannot attempt a further guess,
for of all the acquaintances we have in common, I do not know any one likely to be
here."

"Well then, it was Miss Gay."

"Miss Gay !" he exclaimed with surprise,
so unfeigned, that it caught Lady Cecilia's ear.

"What is that you are telling Mr. Thornton?" said she, turning round, with a peculiar expression of countenance.

"I understand that Miss Gay is here?" he replied, inquiringly.

"Yes," said her ladyship, coldly, "she leaves to-morrow morning."

Thornton interpreted Lady Cecilia's manner to mean, "she will leave to-morrow morning, because she has heard that you are expected." So he replied, "I shall leave by this evening's express."

Mrs. Redford had gathered from the source to which she frequently had recourse, namely, her servants, that Lady Cecilia Mowbray had come to meet her husband; and she recollected having heard from Mr. Redford that Mr. Thornton had accompanied him on his tour abroad. She thought it, therefore, probable that they might return together.

This anticipation induced her to dress with unusual care, and to parade the walk in front of the Hotel, about the time the boat was expected. Consequently, she met Mr. Thornton just as he was entering the Hotel precincts.

She affected surprise at seeing him.

"Is Redford here?" he inquired.

"No; but my mother is, and we expect him every day. I hope you will dine with us this afternoon."

"No, I thank you; I shall leave by the night train. Can you tell me where Miss Gay is staying?"

Her heart beat within her. She was a prey to anger, jealousy, and fears. The shortness of Thornton's manner, really proceeding from excitement, she attributed to some communication that had passed between him and Laura.

"Miss Gay, you know," said she, somewhat scornfully, "is no friend of mine; but

I have heard she is living with a Mrs. Jenkins, a singular sort of person, somewhere on the Cliff."

Thornton, in his turn was irritated and annoyed by her manner, and wishing her good bye rather brusquely, entered the coffee-room, and soon procured a man to conduct him to Mrs. Jenkins's house upon the Cliff.

He had seen Mrs. Owen's death in the papers, and had returned to England with the full intention of seeking out Laura, to offer her his personal condolence, in the hope of rendering it more acceptable than a written one. Lady Cecilia's manner was not encouraging: still he hoped against hope, so strong was his longing for a reconciliation.

Before he reached the gate that opened on the little plot before Mrs. Jenkins's house, he perceived a figure in deep mourning, whose identity he could not mistake, apparently purchasing a basket of shell flowers, for a little girl by her side.

His heart beat so tumultuously, that he could hardly breathe, and as he approached and swung open the gate, the young lady in black looked round, and suddenly turned to enter the house.

In the rush and confusion of his feelings he could not speak—he could only follow her. He could not tell what sentiments towards him, her momentary glance bespoke. By way of regaining his composure, he dismissed his guide. The door had closed upon Laura; the little girl still stood there, her attention divided between himself and her basket of shell flowers.

Thornton rang the bell; it was answered immediately by Williams, who said that Miss Gay was not at home to any one but Lady Cecilia Mowbray.

Thornton recognized the old butler, and taking out a card, wrote hastily on the

back with his pencil; "you do not then
even permit me the privilege of a common
acquaintance? You forbid me to tell you
how deeply I condole with you, how sincerely
I sympathize in your grief." Then doubling
it up, he bade Williams give it to his
mistress.

It was received by her at the door of her
apartment, and instead of tearing it up after
reading it, as she might have been expected
to do, she carefully placed it in a corner
of her writing case, where it remained undisturbed for several months.

Thornton left Folkestone, as he had said
he would, by the evening express, and re-
installed himself in his Albany rooms, whose
unpromising gloom well harmonized with
the dull, hopeless constancy of his passion
for Laura. There he occupied himself in
digesting the materials for thought which he
had gathered during his recent excursion.
He applied himself to the study of documents

bearing upon commercial morality, and the condition of the multitude; and thus he led a life of intellectual labour, of privation, and of moral probation too severe for the virtue of most young men, and not likely to be coveted by many.

Nevertheless, "sweet are the uses of adversity," to those who can profit by them, and probably, now, Thornton looks back upon the long toil and gloom of those winter months, spent in the solitude of deserted London, as one of the best seed-times of his life.

On the following morning Laura, too, departed, leaving Mrs. Jenkins and her household in a state of boastful regret, to talk for days of her afflictions and her fortune, her affability, and the simplicity of her habits and manners. Mrs. Jenkins mentioned to her husband, the report that had been current in her kitchen, respecting Miss Gay's unrequited love, and the bribe; but like a strong-minded woman, she coincided with his exclamation, almost before he had uttered it. "It cannot be true, because it is impossible; for she is only just of age," and thus this piece of gossip, having served the purpose of its inventor, was totally discredited on good authority, like many similarly malicious reports.

Mrs. Redford's visit to Folkestone, also, terminated soon afterwards; for Redford returned from his shooting excursion, to take his wife home, where he was expecting a party of sportsmen for his pheasants; indeed, he had gone to the Highlands rather to make the acquaintance of these friends, than for the sake of grouse shooting.

The Mowbrays remained a short time longer at Folkestone; and then, they too, left to pay their annual visit to Mr. Mowbray, senior, a large-acred squire of Northamptonshire.

Laura, as our readers will remember, had resolved to waste no more time in self-condolence, or in vain dreams of unattainable happiness. Together with the lost possibility of such happiness, she strove to lay aside the desire for it. She was now to commence an active life, with the utmost usefulness for its object, duty for its principle, and cultivation and health for its means. This was, indeed, a grand programme of good resolutions; and like all those who propose to themselves such a career, Laura frequently felt, almost to despondency, her feebleness in accomplishing it; nor, amid all the studious cares of balancing right and wrong, better and worse, for the purpose of action, could she always banish from her memory the secret recollection of brighter days, when sympathy and affection were at hand to kindle and to guard the sacred fires of youthful enthusiasm. Yet such regrets, natural as they are, enervate the mind, and prove a very thorn in the flesh to those who feel them acutely.

When Laura had invited Miss Owen to pay her usual autumnal visit, in compliance with her dear aunt's dying request, it occurred to her that she might, possibly, be glad to remain with her entirely, and thus spare her the necessity of finding a companion. But the notions she had formed of this elderly spinster were not agreeable. They had never, hitherto, spent much time together; for, during Miss Owen's visits, Laura and her father had generally been at Sexhurst; but whenever she had been staying at the Dell with Miss Owen, Laura had avoided her, and left her entertainment to her aunt—herself impressed with awe by her tall, gaunt sister-in-law; whose better birth, and more dogmatic form of evangelism imposed not a little upon her own timid nature. Both the sisters were Low Church, but they pronounced their Shibboleth differently. In the mouth of the one, it conveyed ideas of peace and superabundant mercy; in that of the other, ideas of election, separation, a peculiar people, the mysteries of the apocalypse, the vials of wrath, and the terrors of everlasting damnation.

Such were Laura's impressions of Miss Owen, but they were no longer altogether correct. Miss Owen was becoming resigned to the privations of an unbeloved existence. She still worked indefatigably for missionary baskets, confined her reading to evangelical and anti-Romanist publications; and Laura was sometimes, it is true, shocked by the bad taste and narrow-mindedness of her opinions.

As the two virgins sat working in the evening, after an early tea, occasionally interchanging words, rather than ideas, Laura would silently observe the wrinkles that long disappointment had furrowed on the face of her guest. Her complexion and dull,

grey eye seldom brightened with pleasure,
and only changed into an irritable glow and
nervous twinkle when religion, matrimony,
or love were alluded to.

Sometimes Laura would wonder whether,
unendowed by nature, as Miss Owen must
have been from childhood, a better fate had
been possible to her; and she would inwardly
note the resemblances, and the differences,
both so striking, between her own position
and that of her guest. Her compassion
and sympathy became excited, and her
manners assumed something of the tenderness we show to the frailties of our own
blood relations, or to the irritability of an
invalid.

Miss Owen was on her good behaviour;
for she greatly valued the privilege of a
month's visit to the old haunts of her
childhood, dreary as that had been, under
the auspices of her worldly parents. She
was not destitute of the power of loving;

and her attachments, repulsed by *persons*, were lavished on *places*, and on a visionary future, where retribution and compensation would be the order of the day. She had come prepared to endure the pride, indifference, and levity which she considered the natural attributes of an unregenerated young heiress. She was, therefore, very agreeably surprised by Laura's simple kindness of manner, and touched, in spite of herself, by a certain tone of grave and quiet sorrow, which seemed to be ever present with her.

One evening, as the two sat at work together, Miss Owen said, in an awkward nervous way,

"I hope, Miss Gay, my being here is not disagreeable to you, and that I don't keep you from seeing pleasanter society."

Laura replied, with a look of surprise:

"On the contrary, your society is a

comfort to me. I am not nearly so lonely as I should be without you. You know you are the only living link between myself and the past."

"Well, my dear," said the old lady, blinking, and almost bridling with pleasure, "if I can be of any use to you—if I can in any way add to your happiness—I really am very much obliged to you, my dear, for asking me here, to see the old place, and for treating me so well."

Laura rose to hide a tear; for this little outburst of real gratitude came upon her unexpectedly; and she brought out her aunt's recommendation, that she would always treat Miss Owen with confidence and kindness, for *her* sake, and placing the letter open before her guest, she kissed her forehead, and said:

"You will see there, dear Miss Owen, that you are really here, in your own right. When the month's stay has expired,

I shall ask you to favour me with your company at Sexhurst for another month; and if you accept my invitation, I shall think you very kind, and be much obliged to you."

So attractive was Laura's appeal, and so novel did such treatment seem to Miss Owen, that it awoke within her the whole soul of love. A maternal instinct sprung up in her heart; nature burst the bonds of fate, and Laura became her darling, the delight of her eye, and the charm of her life.

Laura knew well how to assure and to repay her affection; a fine tact, improved by culture and by sorrow, taught her how to converse intelligibly and agreeably with her companion, whose spirit came forth, at the bidding of friendship, into the open air and genial sunshine of real life, according to the will of its Creator.

Both ladies commenced their companionship and joint life, with a feeling of liberty as to its duration; they observed a tacit compact, not to discuss subjects uninteresting to either, and to respect each other's independence of action. The actual result, however, was, that Laura's will became practically supreme as regarded their mode of life, for Miss Owen, never finding herself opposed in matters of opinion, and being uniformly treated by Laura with great respect and affection, naturally acquiesced in all her projects, and sometimes felt even more interested in this success than Laura herself.

CHAPTER II.

SEXHURST, originally, no doubt, Saexans-
hörst, or Saxon's coppice tufted eyrie, over-
looked a populous, long chimney'd village,
through which a large stream, almost a river,
flowed. The broad and picturesque vale was
studded, here and there, with factories, new
churches, dissenting chapels, and schools,
with now and then, a smart little villa, or an
ambitious file of uniform new cottages struggling up the hill on the opposite side of the
valley ; whilst just outside the domain of Sex-

hurst, nestled on one side the old parish church and vicarage, and on the other, at a somewhat greater distance, the new elegant mediæval Catholic chapel, with its uniform dependencies of seminary and Priest's house.

Sexhurst itself, nearly on the summit of a low hill, that stood sentinel to a long barren ridge behind, was built of the same grey stone as the old parish church and the new Catholic chapel; and its wide old-fashioned front, backed by luxurious old trees, and embosomed in evergreens, seemed to afford a benignant patronage to the neighbours on both sides, and to proclaim the beauty of olden times to the utilitarians congregated in the vale below.

But they regarded it now, without envy, for ever since Mr. Gay had purchased it, it had been like a candle set on a hill, beaming forth, to all passers by, order, beauty and cleanliness; to the surrounding denizens, peace and good will, and a desire, the humblest well appreciated, to let them share as far as practicable, in the pleasures its ample grounds and plantations afforded.

Suddenly, indeed, its inward virtues seemed to have betaken themselves to a still more active manifestation; for almost daily, through the late autumn, winter and spring, the parish priest, his brother of the mediæval ritual, the dissenting minister, the schoolmasters and school-mistresses, with now and then some excellent well known Quakeresses, and, best of all, the lady of Sexhurst herself, might be seen ascending and descending, like the angels on Jacob's ladder.

Do not infer, gentle reader, that its fair owner was all things to all men, in a latitudinarian sense; no, her religious faith was fixed, and her own peculiar property; her charity alone was Catholic, and it made her *something* to all men.

Do not imagine either, that she always

came down her hill provided, like a Lady
Bountiful, with a heavy purse full of shillings
and sixpences, and returned with it empty.
Such was not the case—her charity did not
consist in almsgiving — she was not an
accessory to the parish overseer; no, she
took down a heart full of sympathy, and a
head full of good sense, and she brought
home a heart full of sober devotion, and a
head full of humane experience.

Those who applied to her, received encouragement and co-operation, it is true, in
proportion to their single-mindedness, and
the nature of their efforts.   Often times,
also, when they entered the noble old
entrance hall, which occupied the centre of
the house, and now formed a spacious well-
stored library, with some party or sectarian
grievance rankling in their bosoms, obscur-
ing all light except on one minute point,
they would quit it again, refreshed in spirit by
the wide view of the harvest before them,

and the still wider, ever expanding view of those eternal laws of justice and mercy, which few of us question, but which, yet, alas, we too often neglect, for tithes of mint and cummin.

One morning, soon after their arrival at Sexhurst, a servant in gay gold-laced livery might be seen, riding a handsome grey, up the carriage drive.

"How smart that livery looks here," remarked Miss Owen, "yet one would hardly notice it in London."

"Very true," said Laura, "it belongs to the Simkins's, people of more distinction and importance, here, than many richer, better bred people in town. They are the largest manufacturers in the vale, and employ something like twelve hundred hands."

"How horrible!"

"Why horrible?" said Laura smiling, the Simkins's are, upon the whole, flourishing prudent people; they built yonder pretty

Baptist Chapel, on the opposite side of the valley, and the capacious school-room adjoining. They subscribed largely to our parish schools. Their hands are amongst the best dressed attendants at our church, and at the Dissenting chapels. Mr. Simkins and his sons are teetotalers, and so are many of their hands. Those neat cottages running up the hill-side, are the habitations and property of some of their best work-people.

"But they are such vulgar people; and it is shocking to think of a man of that sort having so much power."

"Have you ever been over a woollen or cotton factory? Mr. Simkins has both; and if you like, we will go over them some day."

At this moment, a note was brought in by the servant.

"It is an invitation to dine, next week, with Mr. and Mrs. Simkins."

" Which of course you cannot accept, my
dear Laura. The Simkins's may be all very
well in their place ;—but such excessively
vulgar people—you really cannot associate
with them."

" Yes, I shall accept it for myself; and I
should be glad to do so for you also. If
the Simkins's are vulgar people, and we
are not, that is the very reason why, as near
neighbours, we should associate with them.
Besides, there are young people there, upon
whom, if we are really their superiors in
station, our society may exert a favourable influence. Consider also the multitude under their power. Just now,
you were shocked to think of it. Yet
this multitude, and that power only become dangerous and self-destructive, when
people like ourselves, having the consideration of the masters, indulge in the
pride and petty fastidiousness of a vain
refinement, and keep aloof from them.

Remember the story of the good Samaritan, whose neighbourly kindness knew no distinction of birth or class. I see, too," continued Laura, with a smile, and glancing at the bottom of the note, "that we are invited to meet Lord Flaxley."

"Lord Flaxley! dear me, what can he have to do with the Simkins's? Poor dear Lady Flaxley! she was a great friend of my mother's and of mine, too. We used to attend the same church, and go together to the May Meetings at Exeter Hall. Well, my dear, if you wish it, I will go most certainly."

"Lord Flaxley is come down to canvass the borough," Laura replied, as she accepted the invitation; "and as the Simkins's are the most influential people here of the liberal, or, indeed, of any party, he will no doubt stay with them."

"What sort of girls are the Miss Simkins's?"

" Handsome, lively, and accomplished, with a pronunciation the very reverse of Yorkshire."

" Dear me! if Lord Flaxley should fall in love with one of them."

" He might do worse," said Laura, " than marry a handsome woman with a good fortune, and a great desire to make herself agreeable."

" But only think what a mother-in-law to introduce in town."

Laura laughed heartily, and said, " well, I am not prepared to advocate such a match, on either side. I know nothing of Lord Flaxley's taste, spirit, or circumstances; and, as a general rule, I think women are happier when they marry men in their own rank."

" Perhaps, he might fall in love with you."

" That is not very likely; it is difficult for a man to fall in love with one who gives him no encouragement, and no opportunity of doing so."

So great did Miss Owen's curiosity become, respecting the Simkinses, and the probable conduct of their dinner-party, that for the first time, since they had lived together, Laura found herself constantly interrupted during her morning hours of study, by Miss Owen's perpetual surmises and anticipations. At length, by way of a sop to her impatience, she proposed to go over the cotton-mill. Young Simkins, an active clever young fellow, who had just returned from the university where Prince Albert graduated, did the honours of the place. He would have been passing polite to Miss Gay, had she not, by her manner, given him to understand, that Miss Owen was a person of importance, on whose sole account they had come to see the mill.

The noise, the smell, the rapid motion,

and the brightness of the machinery; the
stout, clean, quick appearance of boys and
girls, and the songs of the latter, bewildered
Miss Owen; and Laura found herself
obliged to ask those questions which might
elicit a general description of the process
of manufacture, and the condition of the
work-people.

Miss Owen was delighted with the excitement of the scene, and the attentions
of the young mill-owner.

They met Mr. Simkins, *père*, in the course
of their perambulations, and after exchanging only a few words with them, because, in
his modesty, he fancied such fine ladies could
not understand him, he passed on, and
young Simkins thought it necessary to
deplore the vulgarizing tendency of constant
association with the mill hands.

Laura merely remarked, " human powers
are very limited, and it is impossible for one
individual in one class, to cultivate them in

every direction.   For my part, I consider
your father a great benefactor, and I admire
his industry and the attention he bestows
upon his work-people."

When they had got into the carriage,
Miss Owen remarked :

"I think you were rather severe with
young Mr. Simkins. He made that remark
respecting his father, out of consideration
for us."

" That was not to his credit His
first consideration is due to his father, to
whom he owes everything he values."

At last, the day for the dinner party
came, and Miss Owen and Miss Gay
were ushered into a luxuriously furnished
drawing-room, fragrant with the choicest
exotics, and lighted up into a perfect
blaze. A harp, a guitar, a concertina, a
piano, and a flute bespoke the musical
tastes of the young people. Statuettes,
bronzes, Bohemian glass, and Parisian

articles of vertu lay scattered in every
direction. Mrs. Simkins, a motherly-look-
ing body—got up regardless of expense,
by the provincial dress-maker and milliner,
presented an uncommon picture of incon-
gruities; on the present occasion her manners were fluttered by nervousness, and
her conversation, in which the dialect of
Yorkshire, and the more recently acquired language of her children strove
for predominance, told how uneasy she felt.
Nothing, however, could exceed her
activity. She moved from chair to
chair, whispered directions to her handsome well-dressed girls, just to show
Miss Owen this or that, or to take care
of Lord Flaxley, who only desired to
make himself agreeable to everybody.

Laura was talking to Mr. Simkins
in a quiet gentle tone, that made him
insensibly decrease the usual loudness of
his own voice, when Mrs. Simkins came

up, and said, without considering that
Lord Flaxley was close behind her.

"I was thinking, I would ask Lord
Flaxley to take you in to dinner, Miss
Gay, and Miss Owen and my husband
could go together."

"What a beautiful double camelia, is
it not? quite a new sort," said Laura
blushing, and turning with Mrs. Simkins
to the corner of the room where the
camelia stood, she then continued in a
low voice.

"If you will take my advice, I should
recommend you to send my friend Miss
Owen into dinner with your eldest son,
whose attentions the other day quite won
her good opinion: as for Lord Flaxley,
I am sure he hopes to take you in,
and I should infinitely prefer accompany-
ing Mr. Simkins."

"Oh! very well; thank you, my dear
Miss Gay," and returning to her husband,

she whispered that Miss Gay wished him to take her in, to dinner.

" Thad's raight !" he exclaimed in stentorian tones, rubbing his hands with satisfaction.

Mrs. Simkins, then proceeded to intimate her wishes on the same subject, to the rest of the gentlemen present. After some delay, dinner was announced, and with a few hesitations and mistakes as to precedence, the whole party sat down in tolerable order. The table was overladen with all sorts of dainties, and rich viands—the dinner was, in fact, what Lord Flaxley called it, " a monstrous spread ;" the wines were various and costly. Mrs. Simkins's civilities to Lord Flaxley were quite overpowering. There were several pauses in the entertainment, and during one of these, Laura heard Lord Flaxley say, in reply to some remark of the hostess.

"Ah! your third son is in the navy—a noble profession."

"That's what I said to his father, says I, the lad knows his own mind best, but because you like spindles, it's no reason he should, besides, I said, don't you know, that we Britons are the tridents of the ocean."

"Capital—capital! upon my word, you are a true patriot, Mrs. Simkins," he replied, with difficulty moderating his laughter to an admiratory pitch.

His eye wandered down the table in search of some one who could share the joke: it traversed without compassion, the down-cast glances of the two Miss Simkins's, and met Miss Gay's, across whose features an unconscious smile had just passed; now she blushed, and looking him full in the face, with a slight, a very slight expression of contempt, seemed to say,

"So you did not know what to expect, and your politeness gave way."

"Thus," thought his lordship, " a good story falls dead to the ground among my stupid and hospitable constituents."

" Who is the young lady sitting near your father," he inquired, addressing the youngest of the Miss Simkins's.

" Oh ! she is Miss Gay," she replied, in a low voice, " she is a great heiress, and so learned."

" Ah ! indeed, Miss Gay ? 1 have a letter of introduction to her, from a mutual friend. This is not the first time I have heard her praises. She is a very accomplished person, I believe."

" Yes," said the young lady, doubtfully looking up, " she is rather accomplished. We do not know her very intimately, but I believe she hardly sings or plays at all. I don't know whether she draws; I should think she did."

"Has she any political influence ?"

"I don't know."

After dinner, Lord Flaxley learned from Mr. Simkins, that Miss Gay, next to himself, could, if she chose, control the greatest number of votes, "but," added he, "I don't think she would allow her name to be used to solicit a vote."

"I think I must call upon her to-morrow. I have an introduction from some friends of hers. Perhaps, I might induce her to approve of my politics."

"I dare say she does so, already," replied Mr. Simkins. "Her father was on the Liberal side, and she follows him in everything."

"Will you do me the favour to introduce me," said he, as they left the dining-room.

Laura was talking to the eldest daughter of the house. The hostess, and the rest of her lady guests were engaged in the entertainment of Miss Owen, who had become quite a personage amongst them, because she had known Lord Flaxley's " poor mother."

On the entrance of the gentlemen, all the ladies became silent, and none seemed to know what next was to be done. Lord Flaxley was presented to Miss Owen. She was so unlike her former self, that he had to apologize for not having recognized her sooner, and he remarked in an insinuating way, that the air of Yorkshire seemed peculiarly favourable to female beauty. He induced her to ask for music, and then left her, to obtain an introduction to Miss Gay.

" I have the honour of already knowing Miss Gay, by report," he remarked: "and this evening, I am but anticipating the pleasure I hope to enjoy to-morrow; for I have brought a letter from our mutual friend, Lady Cecilia Mowbray, to you," bowing to Miss Gay.

"I shall be glad to see any of Lady Cecilia's friends," Laura replied. "Do you know her well?"

"I am only her first cousin."

"They are coming to stay with me soon."

"I wish they were here now, to plead my cause, and induce you to give me some of the votes of which I am informed ·you can dispose."

"They would hardly try to persuade me to interfere with my tenantry in that respect, were they aware that I consider that I have no right to do so."

"But you know, Mowbray is quite in favour of the representation of property, which its possessors now practically enjoy through the unsystematic operation of our constitution; therefore, I think he would urge you to exert your political influence on principle."

" I suspect he would consider my sex a disqualification."

" What! the husband of Lady Cecilia, hold so barbarous a notion? you wrong his good sense."

" Not at all," said Laura, laughing. " I know he is not the politician to be influenced by individual exceptions; besides, you have forgotten to enquire what my political opinions may be; it is evident that you expected me to exercise my power in a very feminine sort of way; in fact, as the least intelligent of my tenants might do, in favour of my friend's friend."

" No," he rejoined, with a graver air, " I understood that the late Mr. Gay was of liberal politics, and that you followed his example in all respects."

" That is true," said Laura, seriously, " but those who imagine that he would have confined the future within the past, or that he was illiberal enough to be a mere partizan, are little able to understand my father's principles."

"I met the other day," said his lordship, willing to change the topic, "a great friend of Mowbray's, Mr. Thornton; perhaps you may know him, I fancy there is a similarity of sentiments between you. He has just published rather a clever pamphlet on the commonweal, which he makes out to be more dependent on intelligent and well matured public opinion, and on social habits and manners, than on party politics, or the action of government in this country; and he ends one section of his book, by saying that no future member of any government can ever hope to compete in power with a journal like the "Times," which represents the intelligent opinion of all classes. He remarks that the sphere of distinction, is daily becoming more varied, but also more narrow, and he rejoices at it, as it brings us nearer to that civilization in which all participate, and where each individual consciously acquiesces in the laws of his being, and his own condition, and endeavours to fulfil them perfectly. This he styles, the ambition of merit, and he represents it as the only one consistent with religion and happiness."

Laura had listened with such evident interest, that Lord Flaxley promised to give her the pamphlet the following day.

The carriages were announced. Young Simkins offered his arm to Miss Owen, and Laura might have proceeded alone to her carriage, had not Lord Flaxley been there, so nearly asleep was Mr. Simkins, senior; for his daughter's music every evening, after dinner, was wont to bring him light and pleasant slumbers.

The night was frosty and starlight, and the two ladies sank back in the carriage to enjoy their own reflections. Laura's dwelt with interest on Charles

Thornton; · and with tearful eyes, she said to herself, "yes, I will love him ever, as I love Plato, as I love Cicero, or Dante in their works; and thus I shall recover him, such as he appeared to be in Rome; I do no longer desire to appropriate him to myself," and looking out into the dazzling starry multitude of infinite space, her spirit there sought that expansive affection, which should enable her to love without perturbation. These reveries were suddenly interrupted by the voice of her companion, who having mused with satisfaction on the events of the evening, desired to communicate her impressions.

"They really are very decent people, after all; I believe Mrs. Simkins is a very good woman; she says, it quite grieves her to see that Puseyite church set up in the midst of us, and she quite agrees with me, in thinking the clergyman has a secret connection with the Jesuits at Sexhurst. She wonders, too, that you should encourage the Catholics, my dear."

"She does not understand my reasons for associating with Mr. Gillow," replied Laura; "and I could not explain them t o her. However, to you I will say, that friendly and neighbourly intercourse with him, and the loan of such books as fill my library, are not likely to develop to excess the peculiar spirit of his church."

"Oh, 1 did not know you were labouring for his conversion."

"Nor am I," pursued Laura, with a smile. "I am never ambitious of great results. I ought also to add that he is a scholar and a gentleman, who exercises some influence in the neighbourhood, and these qualities make his society desirable."

"Do you know," said Miss Owen, "everybody thought Mr. O'Conochy's sermon, last Sunday morning, was addressed to you."

"So I fancied myself. The text was

significant in the mouth of our parson. 'Why halt ye between two opinions? If Baal be God, serve him; if the Lord be God, serve him.' He omitted, however, to explain the position held by the church of Baal in the kingdom of Israel, and to state its doctrines and morality; and he quite forgot that all sects of Christians have one common origin, and one common book of law and divinity. He will dine with us to-morrow; and we can discuss the text with him."

"You do not like him, I fear," remarked Miss Owen.

"Yes, indeed, I do—and for his own sake too; for he is a kind-hearted, hard-working parish priest. His wife has pleasant manners, and they manage their schools very creditably."

"Do you like Lord Flaxley."

"He is very young, and I fancy he has thought but little on the realities of life;

until a man has done that, his character is hardly sufficiently formed to attach my esteem or interest."

They had reached home; and exchanging a kind and sleepy kiss, retired to rest.

Laura, much more than Miss Owen, had appreciated and suffered from the vulgarity of their entertainers; for cultivation had increased her sensitiveness, as well as her charity, and rendered her less susceptible to flattery. Those who found it unsuccessful with her, attributed their failure to pride, rather than indifference; and this, more than anything else, impaired her popularity with females like the Simkins's. With the exception of old Mr. Simkins and Lord Flaxley, the party of that evening had voted Miss Owen a pleasanter person than the beautiful owner of Sexhurst.

Lord Flaxley called in good time the following morning to present Lady Cecilia Mowbray's letter, and Mr. Thornton's pamphlet. Both were most graciously received, and the same friendly reception extended to the bearer.

Sexhurt, its fair owner, and her cheerful spacious old library, delighted him. His conversation was lively, and Miss Owen indulged in many conjectures as to the ultimate result of his lordship's visit; especially as he went away, assuring Laura, that neither he, nor his agent would solicit a single vote in her name. He begged she would reward his forbearance, by allowing him to call again, should he happen to be in the neighbourhood during the visit which the Mowbrays were about to make.

When they did come, a few weeks afterwards, they enjoyed themselves exceedingly. The novelty of Miss Gay's self-created position—her usefulness in it—the varied society—the oddities of the people—the insight afforded into the condition of the manufacturing population—and last, not least, the society of the interesting young hostess herself, and the charm of a comfortable, unostentatious home, with an excellent library, were sufficient attraction to make the Mowbrays remember their sojourn at Sexhurst, as a period of great enjoyment.

Laura made no direct inquiries about Thornton; but she gathered, from what Lady Cecilia and Mr. Mowbray dropped concerning him, that his intimacy with the Redfords had almost ceased; that he associated principally with men of literary and political eminence, and that his avocations were wholly of a studious kind. She dared not hope that he often remembered her; and she would still have avoided thinking of him, if she had not believed him less unworthy of a place in her thoughts. The frequent mention of his name in the papers, and in conversation, had almost taught her to hear it without blushing.

The Mowbrays left Sexhurst for London
as soon as the Session commenced; and Mr.
Mowbray returned to his post, but not before
they had been parties to an arrangement
that Miss Owen and Laura would come up
to town in May—Miss Owen to attend the
Meetings of that season, and Laura to enjoy
society under Lady Cecilia's *chaperonage*.

Time glided peaceably on at Sexhurst, in
the usual occupations and society of the
place; the two ladies had become quite
habituated to each other, and either would
have contemplated a separation with pain, for
the very difference of their views, both as
regarded persons and principles, lessened the
monotony of their life, without in the least
impairing their friendship.

They discussed with joint interest the projected pleasures and self-culture to be derived
from their visit to London; they planned the
appropriation of their time; they both agreed
to see the sights of town in such a way as they

had never seen them before; they undertook all sorts of commissions for everybody, and lest anything should be forgotten, Miss Owen took the precaution during the month previous to their departure, always to carry about with her a memorandum book, in which the following, amongst other entries, were recorded :

Varty's school depôt. Selection of school books. Two pounds of best Scotch snuff, for Mr. Gillow. See Nineveh remains in British Museum. Vanilla pods. Ornamental flower-pots.

Towards the end of May they were domiciled in Miss Owen's house in Brook Street, and in compliance with Laura's wishes, her own servants were already there to attend upon them. This arrangement was not disagreeable to Miss Owen; for by way of making some return for Laura's kindness and hospitality, she good-naturedly assisted her in managing her household—

a business for which she had both the
taste and the capacity, so that now, her
authority was not disputed by any of Miss
Gay's domestics, and it was exercised in
conformity with their mistress's plans, all
of which Miss Owen approved upon trial,
and adopted as fixed rules.

CHAPTER III.

CHARLES THORNTON had passed the autumn and winter in assiduous studies, intermingled with a few conversational dinners and evening calls. He had visited and enlightened his constituents: he had been most cordially received and entertained by his own relations, who heartily congratulated him upon his political prospects, and the favourable turn the bank difficulties had taken.

Parliament had opened, and one of the first persons to accost him in the lobby of the House, was Lord Flaxley, the new member for Littleborough.

It was impossible for Charles Thornton to forget that Sexhurst lay near to Littleborough.

"Well," said Lord Flaxley, "what are the odds that the government will last through the Session?"

"Two to one in their favour, I should say, for party feeling out of doors, grows weaker every day, therefore, party consistency in the House will probably fall more and more to a discount; and, provided there be no egregious jobbing, or administrative blundering, and some respect be shewn to the spirit of the day, I think a government, consisting of any party combination, has a good chance of permanency now a-days."

"This is lucky for me, for had I not been born a Whig, I should certainly have become a Tory. What do you think Mowbray advises me to do?"

"To study Blue Books, and attend committees, I should suppose," replied Thornton, with a smile.

"Yes, I understand," said his Lordship, laughing, "study, study, study, the beginning, middle, and end of life, with Mowbray; in fact, he did recommend me to study—yourself."

Thornton looked surprised, and asked "whether he had been proposed as a warning or an example."

"I forgot to ask; however, my unassisted judgment leads me to conclude, as an example; for your pamphlet, which, in my simplicity, I took to be too deep and philosophic for my comprehension, has charmed the fancy of one of the nicest girls I ever met. I believe she agrees in every word of it, and I hope you will forgive me, for having made over the copy you sent me, to her."

Lord Flaxley did not observe the effort

it cost his companion to appear calm; but
Thornton listened, and did not interrupt
him.

" By the bye, I will give you an account
of my canvass—it was vastly amusing, for I
stayed with the great *parvenus* of the neighbourhood, my largest and wealthiest constituent, whose peculiar crotchets, if I can
recollect them all, I feel bound faithfully to
represent. He is a substantial good sort of
man, after all, and his daughters removed to
the atmosphere of fashionable life, might soon
add its graces to their beauty. Poor things!
they are dying to learn the ways of society.
However, by way of compensation, they enjoy
the precious society of the beautiful owner of
Sexhurst—your admirer. Nay, do not colour,
my good fellow! Mowbray himself, says she
is a wonderful girl. I assure you, her approbation is no disparagement to your author-
ship, and Mrs. Simkins, my constituent's
wife, proclaims her a perfect prodigy:—

and she deserves the character, for she can hear the grossest and queerest blunders without a smile. Ah ! I see I am interesting you—remember the owner of Sexhurst is young and beautiful. Her companion, Miss Owen, is old, and no beauty; she used to be, within my recollection, cross-grained, prim, and fanatical, with all a well-born spinster's notions about birth and exclusiveness; now, under Miss Gay's influence, she has become transformed, as Lady Cecilia Mowbray declares, into an excellent example of a cheerful, good-natured, bustling old maid."

"Do you consider Miss Gay, then, among your constituents?" at last interrupted Thornton.

"No ! but by Jove, I tried hard to gain her influence, but all to no purpose; she made me promise, upon my honour, not to use her name to solicit a single vote. I should like to have been at Littleborough when the Mowbray's were staying at

Sexhurst, but the governor took fright, at my description of Miss Gay, and managed to fill the house, so as to require my presence at Helston, during the whole time of their visit. That was a *contre-temps*, was it not? However, I know she is coming up to town in May; she will often be at the Mowbray's, and I hope to meet her there; if the governor only sees her, I am sure he will like her too."

"Do you mean," enquired Thornton, with sickening interest, "that you entertain serious thoughts of — ?"

"Serious thoughts—oh, no! I never entertained any serious thoughts in my life, but there is no knowing what the most trivial thoughts may lead to, if one is once embarked on their current. By way of proving my seriousness, I will promise *you*, of all men most likely to become my rival, that when Miss Gay comes to town, I will get Lady Cecilia

Mowbray to ask you to meet her, and if you make us a crack speech, during her stay, I will secure her a place in the the House to hear it."

Thornton became grave and silent, and Lord Flaxley supposing his mind preoccupied in the consideration of important subjects, and that frivolous conversation was irksome to him, retreated to the smoking-room in search of gayer company.

Charles Thornton went home, for there was no important business before the House that night, and he longed to ponder over all that Lord Flaxley had told him. The unexpected discovery, that Laura still regarded him with interest, although her affections were withdrawn, renewed within him hopes and desires he had been repressing for months. Those long treasured scenes in Rome, where, side by side, the sympathy of their hearts had promised so fair a prospect of happiness; the depth and firmness of her character, the joy that had beamed in her face at the Flower Show, the confusion of her bow, the indignant anguish of her retort, when, loosing the reins of jealous passion, he had cruelly upbraided and repulsed her; all rushed through his memory, and again, as before, he buried his face in his hands and wept. How bitterly had he atoned for one short hour's passion! and how disproportionate his punishment to the offence! Laura, too, had she not suffered? Her continued avoidance of him only proved how deeply. The knowledge that he had endured all this in consequence of a fault, so little habitual to him—for he knew that few men maintained a calmer temper under provocation than himself, and the idea of continuing a life so devoid of gratification to his warmest feelings, and so destitute of all hope of domestic happiness, were intolerable.

Lord Flaxley's careless remarks had given him a ray of hope, that his course of life was not unobserved by Laura, and that, by patient continuance in well-doing, he might at last obtain a re-admission to her society and friendship.

Ever since his landing at Folkestone, he had avoided Lady Cecilia Mowbray, whose wishes he believed to be inimical to his happiness; he had, also, scrupulously shunned Mrs. Redford's society, of whose deep-rooted dislike to Miss Gay he was now convinced; and he no longer doubted, that at the Flower Show, she had gratified her malice by suggesting to his credulous jealousy the false report, and the false interpretation of Laura's behaviour there, which had led to his rupture with her. He did not, he could not, exculpate himself; but he detested his tempter, and thoroughly pitied the man whose wife was so unprincipled and mischievous a woman.

Was it really true, that Laura intended coming up to town in May? Perhaps they might meet—would she recognize him? Would she permit him to address her? But suppose Lord Flaxley, or some other unknown suitor, beset her, how should he compete with him. He was unable to answer these self-suggested queries, and the only result of his anxious cogitations was, a resolution to attend so sedulously to his parliamentary duties, as to keep himself in the minds of those with whom Laura associated, and, above all, to cultivate the Mowbrays' acquaintance. Mr. Mowbray he knew was his friend; with the young people, likewise, he was a favourite; and he entertained well-founded hopes that, thus supported, he might, ere long, win back Lady Cecilia's esteem and regard. Through her, he would seek tidings of Laura, and he trusted that, in the intimate conversations of these ladies, he might not be altogether forgotten. This last was a happy idea, and he spared no effort to insure its success. His friendship with the Mowbrays prospered. Each time she saw him, Lady Cecilia treated him with more and more consideration and cordiality. Still, her suspicions respecting the nature of his intimacy with the Redfords, had not entirely vanished, and before she dismissed them, and restored him to her good opinion, she hazarded an allusion to Mrs. Redford, so far from complimentary, that a *cavaliere servente* must have resented it. His manner and his answer surprised her ladyship. They evinced no feeling of kindness towards Mrs. Redford, of whom he spoke as a heartless and uninteresting woman.

"My intimacy with Mr. and Mrs. Redford," he frankly said, "arose from the belief, perhaps erroneous, that I was under great obligations to Mr. Redford."

Here he stopped so abruptly, as to forbid

any further inquiry, and Lady Cecilia concluded, from his manner, and her own experience of character, that whatever truth there might be in his excuse, he had almost dropped the acquaintance, because he was at length disgusted with Mrs. Redford's coquetry.

Susan Mowbray gave him a description of Laura's occupations and amusements at Sexhurst; her brother described the place and the neighbourhood. From them, too, he gleaned her opinion of Lord Flaxley; and he felt assured that, for the present at least, he had no very formidable rival to fear.

The month of May found Thornton quite re-instated in the good opinion of Lady Cecilia, who resolved, also, to remove the false impressions she had entertained, and first communicated to Laura, on the subject of his connection with the Redfords. She even contemplated an attempt to reconcile the lovers, and to repair the mischief her unwitting repetition of scandal had done.

This, however, did not prove so easy a task as she expected, for Laura gave her but little encouragement to talk about Thornton, and though rejoicing in her heart to hear that a better reason existed for his frequenting Mr. Redford's house, than she had believed, she could not forget what had passed at the Flower Show, nor the careless way in which he must have mentioned the loan, either to Mr. or Mrs. Redford. She felt convinced that she had once deceived herself as to the depth of his affection for her, and she knew, too well, what she had suffered in consequence. It had cost her so much to regain her composure and the free use of all her faculties, that she felt it would be wrong to expose herself to another meeting which might only end in further suffering. She resolutely refused all proposals to join any party, to which he was invited: and Lady Cecilia was obliged to content herself with retracting everything she had told Laura in disparagement of Thornton, and by now telling her everything she knew to his credit.

Laura heard this with secret joy, for it justified the affection for him which she had formed in Rome and could not succeed in banishing from her heart. She began to recur, with a certain pleasure tinged with soft melancholy, to the conversations they had had together in Rome. She thought with satisfaction, that did *he* know it, he must certainly approve the life she was now leading; every sentiment she came across in her reading, that reminded her of him, was reperused and marked. Nay, the card he had left at Folkestone, which lay folded up, in a corner of her desk, was sometimes taken from its hiding place; yet still, with timid obduracy, Laura Gay avoided meeting her lover.

Once, Thornton called before noon to see Mr. Mowbray—a carriage was at the door, and the faithful, the grave, the constant Williams stood beside it, talking to the coachman, " Laura is within!" said Thornton to himself, " Heaven grant that Mr. Mowbray may be out, and then I shall be shown into Lady Cecilia's rooms, we shall meet ;—and in a state of great agitation, he awaited the reply to his knock.

Heaven, for once, was unpropitious, for Mr. Mowbray *was* at home, and very glad to see him, moreover, he was quite ignorant who Lady Cecilia's visitors were, and it never entered his head to suppose that Thornton wished to see them.

Poor Thornton! his colour came and went, his heart beat fast, as he heard the sound of light footsteps on the stairs, and the silver tones of Laura's voice, bidding Lady Cecilia and Susan " good morning."

Nothing of all this did Mr. Mowbray

observe, for in the first place, he was deep in laboriously summing up, and weighing for his young friend's benefit, the facts for and against a proposal then before a committee, upon which they both sat; in the second place, Thornton's eye remained fixed upon Mr. Mowbray, with an expression of the most intense interest, indicative, really, of the breathless attention he was giving to sweeter sounds than Mr. Mowbray could have produced.

The carriage drove off, and Lady Cecilia opened the door of her husband's study. Charles Thornton positively started at her appearance—nor did he perceive the surprise of her greeting; but he *did* notice that her manner to him was uncommonly kind; and he hastily concluded that she knew of his call—that Laura had refused to see him, and that she thought he was hardly used.

" Miss Gay has just left us," said she to

her husband. "She came to ask Susan to accompany her to the Exhibition of Paintings to-morrow morning, before the gallery becomes hot and crowded. I should have been glad to have allowed her to go, were to-morrow not Signor Garcia's singing lesson."

"Ah, well!" sighed Thornton, as he left the house, "it is clear that Laura Gay is cheerful, whilst I am sad. She regards me just as she regards any other person whose opinions she approves. That past, to me so dear, is nothing to her. Would I could equal her indifference; but, I am not the spoiled and beautiful child of fortune. Whilst she treads the green sward of youth, beloved and obeyed, my path through life is rugged and uncheered by affection, and the toil that earns each step I gain, is unconfessed and forgotten by all but myself."

Notwithstanding these gloomy forebodings,

and the desire, in which he believed himself sincere, to become indifferent to Laura, he did not neglect to profit by Lady Cecilia's intimation. Early the following forenoon, regardless of the blazing heat of the streets, he was journeying rapidly towards the National Gallery. Laura had arrived before him. There were only a few straggling groups in the larger room; yet, among them were several female forms, about the height of Laura Gay. At last, his attention was caught by two ladies, standing opposite a large painting of ancient Rome; one was just of Laura's height and figure, the other was tall and lank, and Thornton stood close behind them.

The taller and older lady, said to her companion, "well, my dear, I see nothing particular to admire in that picture."

"Perhaps not, as a picture, but to me, the subject has a peculiar attraction," was the reply, uttered in a tone of tender regret.

"The voice is Laura's, and the sentiment, too. Dear, precious Laura!" murmured Thornton to himself, as the two
ladies passed on. "How shall I approach
you, to bless you, and thank you, for those
sweet words of comfort. You have broken
the barrier, and nothing, now, shall separate
us."

He followed them, at a little distance, into
the further room, but Laura and her companion were so absorbed in examining the
pictures, that they seemed not to notice any
one. He was standing a little behind them,
and somewhat nearer the doorway, when
Lord Flaxley came up, exclaiming in tones
of surprise, "you here, Thornton, why, I
did not suppose you ever indulged in any
sort of recreation."

Lord Flaxley stood between Charles
Thornton and the two ladies. His greeting
had been heard, and Laura turned in-
stinctively towards the speaker.

Thornton stood, regarding her fixedly, and their eyes met. At first, he observed her face suffuse with a blush—the next moment, it became deadly pale, and her head sank on the shoulder of her companion, who hastened to conduct her away. Both Thornton and Lord Flaxley pressed forward to proffer assistance—the former was first at the side of his fainting mistress, but though speechless, she had sufficiently recovered herself gently to motion him away with her hand. She scarcely looked at him, and he had the mortification of hearing her companion say :

" My dear child, take Lord Flaxley's arm, this room is so hot, you will be better when we get into the air."

They passed quietly out of sight. Thornton turned on his heel and stared vacantly at the pictures : their garish colours, the heat of the fast filling rooms, and above all, the failure of his attempt to accost Laura Gay, distressed him so much, that he felt in danger of being reduced to the same predicament as herself. Hardly knowing whither he went, he descended into the sculpture room, and having placed himself opposite the ugliest group there, remained fixed in the attitude of an admirer, a circumstance which tended to vitiate the public taste that day, inasmuch as it caused many ladies and gentlemen, to discover imaginary perfections, and to pass favourable judgments upon the execution of the aforesaid group.

Revolving in his mind Laura's remark, and her excessive emotion at seeing him, he thought he understood it all, she loved him still, in spite of herself, if not, why that sudden and involuntary turn of the head when his name was pronounced? Why the glowing colour of her cheeks? But, still she was deeply offended. She could not, and would not forgive him; therefore, the sudden change of countenance, at encountering his gaze; the disdainful motion of her hand, as with averted face she motioned him off. It was misery to think of Laura, always implacable; it was surpassing delight to know, that he had not ceased to occupy a place in her affections.

The effect of this encounter, was to increase the ardour and constancy of his attachment, and although nothing would even have induced him to seek another meeting in public, he yet hoped, in course of time, fortune favouring, that a reconciliation might be possible. A reconciliation—he could no longer doubt that the signification of that word to him, would be—perfect happiness!

Laura soon recovered herself, as they drove through the air.

"How you frightened us," said Miss Owen, "Lord Flaxley was quite excited, and the stranger who first offered his

arm, was almost as pale as yourself. I
wonder who he was?"

" I can tell you," replied Laura, lan-
guidly looking down. " His name is
Thornton, he is the member for Hyde,
and the author of the pamphlet Lord Flaxley gave me. I used to know him, during
my poor aunt's life-time."

" Poor dear! he reminded you of her,"
said Miss Owen. Laura was silent, and
Miss Owen proceded:

" Ah, my dear, I often perceive, that
you are thinking of that sweet angel. I
little knew what she was during her life-
time, and now, it is too late. She could
hardly love me, as I was then; yet *she*
was always kind and good, whilst *I* was
jealous and proud. No wonder, you should
stop and look at that picture of Rome.
But why did you not remind me what
its attractions were; for now, you know,
I am changed, thanks to your friendship,

my darling. Now, I think of your dear aunt as a model of Christian goodness. You must never fear talking to me about her."

Laura pressed her hand in reply.

When they reached home, Miss Owen wished Laura to go to her own room, the coolest and quietest in the house, and rest there until it was time to dress for dinner. Indeed, she would wilingly have persuaded her to give up the idea of dining in Eaton Square, with the owners of Llanbeddwr.

Laura declared herself so much better, that no such self-denial was requisite; and prevailed on Miss Owen to leave her alone, and to go out for the purpose of executing some of the numerous commissions still uneffected.

Solitude was a necessary restorative to her agitated nerves; and, from the meditations it permitted, she hoped to derive sufficient strength and presence of mind to make another such deplorable exhibition of weakness impossible. She deeply lamented to think, that once again, and after so long an interval, and so many struggles, her emotion should have confessed so much attachment to one who had long ceased to love her—for that such was the case, she had not a doubt. On that supposition alone, could she account for his hard brusque manner, when first they met, on her return from Rome, or his silence afterwards, until, by accident, he found her at Folkestone. His visit of condolence there, perhaps, signified a willingness to be on terms of civil acquaintance, such as should remove the awkwardness of finding themselves guests together in the same house.

Laura had heard, that very morning from her maid, of Thornton's call at Mr. Mowbray's.

"So, ma'am," said Mrs. Slater, "you'd an agreeable surprise yesterday, seeing Mr. Thornton again."

"Mr. Thornton? where?"

"Well, really, Williams could not be mistaken though, I should think. He told me, as Mr. Thornton called at Mr. Mowbray's, just as you was gone in there; and he looked so hard at him, that Williams touched his hat; and the gentleman knew him, and looked as much as to say, "Oh, so you're still living with Miss Gay."

"No doubt he was calling upon Mr. Mowbray."

"Well, I used to think Mr. Thornton every inch a gentleman in Rome; but I think he's got so many high and mighty notions, now he's an M.P. that he don't suit my taste. I think, he might have asked to see you, ma'am, even if he was a-going to discuss the affairs of state with Mr. Mowbray. It would not have wasted such a deal of his precious moments, I should think."

Laura concluded that this was a proof of complete indifference to her; for, had he wished to see her, he might have asked for Lady Cecilia. Had he dreaded meeting her, he would have left his card, and not entered the house where she was. She could not contemplate their relative positions without the greatest humiliation. She was persuaded that he had understood her assurances on the Veii road. The very words in which he had reclaimed his Shakespeare, proved that he recognized and wished to break a tacit engagement; and now she had [the mortification of thinking that he possessed the further secret of her constancy.

Concerning one of the disagreeable incidents consequent on the rupture of her engagement with him, she was sorely puzzled, having, recently, received a letter of thanks, from Charles Thornton, who had paid off the whole of the loan; for, if the letter were sincere, and it had a great air of sincerity, he certainly did not suspect *her*, of being his friend in need. She took it of her writing-desk, and again thoughtfully reperused it.

"Good fortune has enabled me to repay the whole of your generous loan, sooner, perhaps, than you or I could have expected, but neither time, nor fortune will ever enable me, sufficiently to express the gratitude, I must always feel to one, whose confidence in me has been so implicit, and whose interest has been so sincere. In vain, have I sought to discover you, my benefactor. If it be you, as for a time I suspected, the friend of my boyhood, why have you so well dissembled your kindness? If, as I have latterly supposed, I am in utter ignorance of my benefactor add this further boon to your generosity and discover to me now, the rare and liberal man, the possession of whose friendship would only lay me under deeper obligations."

The idea struck her, for the first time, that Charles Thornton considered himself indebted to Redford for the loan. This would explain Lady Cecilia's present and former impressions; and Mrs. Redford's beauty, vanity, and coquetry, were quite sufficient to give a colour to the scandal current last summer, respecting her intimacy with Thornton. The more Laura reflected on the matter, the more persuaded she was, that, at last, she had arrived at the true interpretation of his conduct, so far as the Redford's were concerned, and the more she regretted that the blind sophistry of passion should have roused her jealousy, and deprived her of calm self-possession on the day of the Flower Show. Had she exercised her reason then, she might have replied less indignantly to Thornton in the refreshment tent ; perhaps, she might have received his call at Folkestone—explanations might have followed, and perhaps—oh, no— no more perhaps's—again they were following the current of vain desires. The past could not be altered, and she was not the girl to resign herself to present evils, because they had a root in the past. Determining, therefore, no longer to shun Charles Thornton; she would meet him, in his own way, as a mere acquaintance. She would bow whenever they met, and accustom herself to speak to him, as to any other of her acquaintance.

Miss Owen was really glad, on her return, to find Laura looking well enough and composed enough to accompany her to Eaton Square, for she felt rather nervous at the idea of Mrs. Owen's patronizing and somewhat slighting air, if Laura were not there to enforce politeness.

Mr. Owen had, in childhood, been brought up in narrow circumstances. His father and mother were people of birth, possessing the traditions of gentility; and the little society they could afford, was composed, for the most part, of well-connected families like their own, of limited fortune and rather contracted education. While yet a minor, Mr. Owen had become the heir of Llanbeddwr, and to his praise be it recorded, that he was as anxious as his parents, to fit himself for the wider sphere and larger fortune whch awaited him; but the period of life between seventeen and twenty-one is rarely fruitful in results to those who have yet to master the elements of a liberal education, and young Owen was not the youth to overcome common obstacles of this kind. He was good-natured and quiet, with no expensive tastes or habits, but without talent or knowledge of the world. He was a man of honour, so far as he understood the meaning of the term, and he readily acquiesced in promising to repay the sums advanced by his relatives and friends to send him to Cambridge. There, he really did his best, and by dint of cramming and study that made him ill, he succeeded in passing his 'little go,' and in due time, received his degree, a distinction which, as it was formerly conferred, proved rather the charity of the examiners, than the acquirements of the scholar. At Cambridge, young Owen was conscientiously frugal, and his chief friend there was Lord Huntley, whom he visited during the long vacation, and whose sister he married almost as soon as he entered into possession of his property.

She was young and very pretty and very simple when she became Mrs. Owen. She, too, was of a numerous, though noble family, brought up in forced seclusion and in straightened circumstances. Lord Huntley had done all in his power for his younger brothers and sisters, but he inherited a heavily mortgaged and ancient estate, yielding not much income beyond the family living.

The first two years of Mr. and Mrs. Owen's married life were spent on the continent, chiefly in Italy. There, they acquired a taste for the arts, some tolerable copies of the Old Masters, and some intolerable soi-disant originals: besides this, they learned how to spend money, how to value fine acquaintances and a social position, and, on their return to England, they devoted themselves and their wealth to the cultivation of society, with as much ability as they possessed. In pursuance of this object, Mr. Owen became member for the county; and Mrs. Owen was ever changing in manners, voice, habits, opinions, and dress, according to the highest models within her reach. At one time, she was sprightly and energetic; at another, languid, indifferent and drawling. Diamonds and lace, a box at the opera, and a larger establishment of servants than she could either manage or employ, became indispensable. Their entertainments were characterized by a style quite in advance of the fashion of her guests, who themselves marked the transitionary state of her society, for they were gathered from a variety of sets. Had she not been young and pretty, Mrs. Owen would often have appeared ridiculous; and had not valuable slate quarries been discovered near Llanbeddwr, the young couple would have been certainly ruined. As it was, they always lived up to their increasing income.

Such were the host and hostess, into whose drawing-room in Eaton Square, Laura and Miss Owen were ushered. The party was, on this occasion, rather more mixed than usual, for the hostess was in doubt as to Miss Gay's and Miss Owen's position in society. The gentleman introduced to Laura, to conduct her to dinner, was a Mr. Brocklebank, a retired and wealthy merchant and ship-owner, an M.P., and an influential director of one of the great railway companies.

Mr. Owen had been strongly advised by his man of business, and by the North Wales Junction Railway Company, consisting at the time of our story, of an engineer, a lawyer, and a secretary, to cultivate Mr. Brocklebank's society and good will, in order that he might be induced to support an arrangement of purchase or guarantee on behalf of the great company he represented, of the North Wales Junction Railway Company; which depended chiefly for traffic upon Mr. Owen's slate quarries. This fact was not stated in the prospectus of the new company, and more than that, its directors and shareholders were merely nominal, and it could hardly be expected, when constructed, to defray its working expenses unless taken up as a feeder by some powerful neighbour.

It is not to be supposed, that Mr. and Mrs. Owen understood this. All they knew about the matter, was, that their agent, under whose care their income had so much increased, recommended them earnestly to cultivate Mr. Brocklebank's society; and also to invite to meet him, Mr. Dillon, a gentleman-like and plausible parliamentary agent. The latter had arrived rather early, and had given a hint to Mr. Owen not to invite Mr. Brocklebank down to Llanbeddwr.

Miss Gay and her cavalier liked each other's looks, and soon became engaged in conversation.

"Pardon me," said he, "but you remind me of a gentleman I knew very many years ago, before your time, I dare say, whose name was the same as yours. He was my senior, and at that time, I considered him the model of what an English merchant ought to be, strictly honourable and truthful, and, though naturally reserved, sincere and liberal in all his dealings."

"That was my father," said Laura, a glow of filial tenderness and exaltation illumining her countenance, "I had the misfortune to lose him about two years ago."

"You will be glad to know that the junior partners, who bought your father's business when he retired, are men of probity and intelligence, who maintain the old character of the firm. Your father's judgment in choosing his clerks, and his firmness and discretion in training them well fitted them to succeed him."

Laura was delighted with Mr. Brocklebank, and he was equally charmed with her, for she had beauty, sense, and youth, a parentage he deemed a guarantee of noble qualities, and a filial piety, which he, as a parent, could not fail to estimate highly.

Mr. Brocklebank's countenance was shrewd, but perfectly honest; his bearing and manners, independent and hearty.

Laura soon found out, in conversation,

what place he was member for, what party he supported, how few people present he knew, how slight and scant his acquaintance with host and hostess was, where he resided in the country, which son was at Eton, and which at Rugby, that the elegant pretty looking girl opposite was his only daughter just come out, and that the decided looking lady, with white hair and a fresh complexion, a little further up the table, was Mrs. Brocklebank, who, he was sure, would have very great pleasure in becoming acquainted with Miss Gay. Laura, in return, communicated Miss Owen's relationship to their host, the connection subsisting between that lady and herself, the fact that they lived together the greater part of the year at Sexhurst, and that she had a pretty little place near Llanbeddwr, where she intended to spend July, August, and September of this year.

" Can you give me a notion of the population thereabouts?" said he.

" Yes, it is exeeedingly thin and scattered, but that is not surprising, for the soil is poor and the cultivation worse."

" Is it not frequented by tourists?"

"No, it does not lie in the beaten track of the beauties of North Wales."

" There are some important slate quarries there, I understand."

" No, I think not, I never heard of any in the neighbourhood."

Mr. Brocklebank smiled, and was silent.

Holding forth *pro bono publico*, on the opposite side of the table, sat Mr. Dillon, the *habitué* of a very popular club; a man who, by hook or by crook, obtained admission into all kinds of houses, where he gathered together all kinds of *on dits*, which he retailed judiciously, according to his company.

To hear him talk, at one table, you would

fancy he associated with gentlemen of the
press; at another, he would seem to be
the favoured guest of the great capitalists;
at another, he would give himself out as
a man of *recherché* pleasures—the two
last were the parts he was playing to-day.
Some one mentioned the name of the
young member for Hyde.

"Thornton!" said he, "I knew him well,
before that foolish and unfortunate attachment for a certain lady. I used to see a
good deal of him, but since I have ceased to
frequent Redford's parties, I rarely meet
him."

Laura's cheeks glowed with shame and
annoyance, and she felt inclined herself to
contradict the calumny; but she was spared
the necessity, for Mr. Brocklebank exclaimed
in a tone of authority:

"Pardon me, Mr. Dillon; there is no
truth in that piece of gossip. It was talked
about last Session for a few weeks, and it

may still be current amongst certain persons
who frequent the lobby of the House, or the
smoking room of your club. Perhaps, when
next you hear it, you will say it has long
since been exploded, as a stupid and mischievous story, and I have the best authority
for asserting that Mr. Thornton had a very
different, and a more worthy and sufficient
reason for his intimacy with Mr. and Mrs.
Redford. I am not," added he in a lower
tone to Laura, "in the habit of voting in
the same lobby with Mr. Thornton, our
politics differ, and my acquaintance with
him is only such as a committee-room, and
observation of his conduct there and in the
House permit, but in the course of my
commercial avocations, I have had a wide
experience of men, especially of young
men, and I am quite sure Mr Thornton is incapable of a criminal or dis-
honourable sentiment. In fact, I happen to
know the real cause of his friendship for

K 2

Mr. and Mrs. Redford, and it is greatly to his credit."

"Indeed," said Laura, deeply interested, "shall I be indiscreet if I ask you to tell me what it was?"

"I owe you a little indiscretion," replied Mr. Brocklebank, with a shrewd smile, "in return for one you have innocently committed in my favour. You have been a good witness against a railway through the Llanbeddwr estate, and perhaps prevented me from selling an important trust, for a mess of potage. If you know Mr. Redford at all, it is not surprising you should ask, how he came by such a friend as Mr. Thornton; but it was thus: "About eighteen months ago Mr. Thornton was involved in pecuniary difficulties, being one of the largest shareholders in a Joint Stock Bank which failed. He was about to make a great and unnecessary sacrifice of other property to meet the demands of the bank creditors, when Mr. Redford interfered

and urged him, with all the zeal of friendship to seek for temporary accommodation,
and even aided him materially in this object.
Mr. Thornton took his friend's advice, and
has ever since felt grateful to him for it."

Before the evening was over, Laura
had invited Mrs. Brocklebank and her
daughter to spend a few days with her at
the Dell. When Mr. Brocklebank came up
and joined the ladies, she was seated near
his daughter.

"Do you know, papa," said the young
lady, " Miss Gay has invited us to spend a
few days with her in North Wales, and mamma
accepts the invitation, if you should be at
liberty at the time Miss Gay has mentioned."

" I will make a point of being at liberty,"
said he, bowing to Laura, and adding,
to his daughter; "shall I tell you, my
dear, how I gained Miss Gay's good
will ?"

His daughter looked up inquiringly, and he added:

"By praising her father."

"By putting down a false report, also," said Laura, "and by adducing the good you knew of an absent person, to disprove a false insinuation against his character."

"I shall enjoy visiting you exceedingly in North Wales. If you are a good walker or rider, we can survey the proposed line of railway, discover the *valuable* quarries, and estimate the probable traffic, but don't tell Owen or Dillon."

"Mr. Owen, I should think," said Laura, laughing, "understood nothing about it, and as for Mr. Dillon, he will never be an acquaintance of mine."

"Don't be too sure. Do you know his *sobriquet*?"

"No."

"Everywhere Dillon! You don't know where you may meet him next; no society that promises plunder is exempt from his intrusion."

When most of her guests were gone, Mrs. Owen considered it requisite to apologize to Miss Gay, for having asked her to meet so mixed a party.

" No apologies are necessary. You could not have asked me to meet more agreeable people than the Brocklebanks."

" I am surprised at your taste," exclaimed Mrs. Owen, " surely you do not profess to like *parvenus*."

" That is quite a misnomer, I think. To my mind, a *parvenu* is one who, by some lucky speculation, or some unexpected inheritance, or some other god-send, falls into a fortune, or a station in life, which he discredits, by his unfitness for it. The *parvenu* is generally conceited and affected; he over-values all the most trumpery distinctions of life; he is insolent to his inferiors, and toadies his superiors. Now, Mr.

Brocklebank's manners bespeak the man
of sense and honour; he is independent,
and contented with the position he has
earned for his family.   To such a man,
wealth, and the responsibilities and trusts,
with which he is invested by his fellow
citizens, are the best titles to the respect of
society. He is no *parvenu*; and if his power
has been obtained in the rough struggles of
life, he holds it by the chivalrous right of
conquest."

Shaking hands with her hostess, and
carried away for the moment by her own
enthusiasm, Miss Gay repeated the following
lines of Burns:

> " The king can make a belted knight,
>   A marquis, duke, and a' that,
> But an honest man's aboon his might,
>   Guid faith he mauna for that.
>   For a' that, and a' that,
>   His dignities, and a' that,
>   The Pith o' sense, and Pride o' worth,
>   Are grander far than a' that."

"What an odd girl that is," remarked Mrs. Owen to her husband, when all the guests had gone; "I cannot imagine how my brother came to admire her."

"I don't know, she never seems odd to me, when we talk together."

"I suppose the men tolerate her because she's so pretty."

"However that may be, it is quite certain; she *is* liked; and by people too, with whom we should be glad to visit."

"By the Mowbrays—oh, yes! I dare say they profess to be literary, and so does she."

"That may be, but what say you to Lord Flaxley, who is no more literary than myself; and yet he would give one of his eyes to get an invitation to Llanbeddwr, while Miss Gay is in the neighbourhood."

"Would he?" rejoined the lady, with increased animation; "then invite him by all means."

" We had better ask some one else, whom he might like to meet; otherwise the pretext would be too barefaced."

" *Et de mauvais goût.* Very well, we will soon find a likely person to meet his lordship."

On the following morning, as Laura and Miss Owen sat at breakfast, the latter remarked.

" I thought a good deal of what you said last night concerning Mr. Brocklebank, and really, I think I agree with you. The daughter is an extremely lady-like girl, and the parents seem highly respectable people."

" You know," replied Laura, " I rate the highly respectable, far before the lady-like; and prefer reality to seeming."

" Did you notice Mr. Dillon? He is a gentleman-like intelligent man, and has the *entrée* to the best society."

" I hope you don't believe a word he told you," said Laura laughing, " for he is not at all a respectable person. He rarely speaks the truth, and I have it on the best authority, that he seeks to enrich himself by swindling the public."

"Oh! how shocking; really, how deceitful appearances are—I should never have suspected it."

"I did."

Thereupon, Laura related to Miss Owen a portion of the conversation between herself and Mr. Brocklebank, and informed her that she had invited the Brocklebank's to spend a few days with them in Wales. The two friends then proceeded to discuss the day of their own departure. Laura was really more anxious to go than Miss Owen, for notwithstanding all her good resolutions, she felt nervous at the idea of again encountering Charles Thornton. She, therefore, suggested that preserving time was at hand, that the fruits of the Dell were most delicious, that the bees would be swarming, and the hay would be making; that in all probability, some little house decorations, and garden arrangements would be necessary before they received the Brocklebanks, and the Mowbrays who were soon to follow them. These prospects of important activity, enchanted Miss Owen, and decided her to forego the gratification of showing to her friends in town, how much she was beloved and esteemed by Miss Gay.

The two ladies were out shopping all the morning, and returning on foot through Grosvenor Square, they were joined by Lord Flaxley, who said he was coming to enquire after Miss Gay. He expressed great delight at seeing her so completely recovered; and talked with so much volubility that they did not perceive, on approaching their own door, that the gentleman who was advancing towards them, had but just quitted it, and it was no other than Charles Thornton. He looked earnestly at Laura as he passed. She coloured deeply, and bowed. Lord Flaxley was on the outside, and nodding familiarly as Thornton went by, he half-whispered in his ear, "all's well that ends well."

Miss Owen invited Lord Flaxley to come in, and take lunch with them; her young friend ran up stairs to take off her bonnet, and to receive the card Thornton had left for her. Unlike the one at Folkestone, it had no writing on the back, and the servant said, the gentleman did not ask for the ladies, but only inquiring how Miss Gay was, desired that his card might be given to her.

"It was a mere call of ceremony, after all," sighed Laura to herself. "Oh! would that I could get rid of my foolish wishes. Some of these days, I really will seek an explanation, whatever pain it may cost me, I will make him assure me, once for all, that he has ceased to care for me—that alone will put an end to my folly."

She was in no mood to be civil to Lord

Flaxley. His perpetual mirth, his easy familiarity, annoyed her, and perhaps she might have exhibited some of this feeling, had she found him alone on her return to the drawing room ; but, to her great surprise, Mr. Dillon was there also.

He had taken Miss Owen down to dinner on the preceding day, and presuming on her relationship to the host, and the impression his attentions had evidently made upon her, had ventured to call, professedly upon Miss Owen, but really upon Miss Gay.

He had evidently made Miss Owen introduce him to Lord Flaxley, and they were now talking together, about a railway scheme, at present under consideration of a committee on which Lord Flaxley sat.

Laura took not the least notice of the intrusive visitor, or of Lord Flaxley either, so long as they conversed together, but retired into the back drawing-room to collect some books.

Mr. Dillon finding, at last, that Lord Flaxley was no longer listening to him, approached Miss Owen, and in a very audible whisper, begged her to present him to her charming niece.

Laura turned round and replied, somewhat disdainfully:

"I am astonished that one, with whom Lord Flaxley condescends to converse, should be so far ignorant of the rules of good breeding, as to ask for an introduction to me in such a way. However, I am glad to see, that you are so slightly acquainted with my friend Miss Owen, as to mistake her for my aunt."

The gentleman was unexpectedly confounded. He had not imagined that two single ladies, of whom the elder was Miss Owen, his neighbour at dinner, would have been so well able to cope with his impudent assurance. Considering himself handsome, and clever, and having ascertained that Miss Gay was a girl of large fortune, without father or mother, he deemed nothing easier or more praiseworthy than to woo and win her. For once in his life, he was completely *déjoué*, and slunk out of the room, with a crest-fallen bow which nobody returned.

Lord Flaxley laughing heartily, inquired who he was.

Laura told him where they had met him the evening before, and why he had been invited there.

"Oh! I will banter Owen on the company he keeps; that is well known to be a tender point with him; and if ever Dillon should be a witness for any scheme in committee, on which I may happen to sit, I shall not forget your account of him."

"The fellow reminded me," continued his lordship, during lunch, "that we had met before, and now I recollect where. The other night, I had a card for a ball in Belgravia, at the next house to Mr. Redford's. Stupidly enough, mistaking the door, I walked into his house, which was open for a *soirée*, and did not discover my error until I reached the drawing-room, where 1 found Mrs. Redford in the full blaze of beauty, supported by two Orientals, Mr. Ballennie, a few literati, and Mrs. Wyndham, whose voice was audible above all others. I did not hesitate to stay a few minutes, to gratify admiration or curiosity. Just as I was on the point of making my *congé*, that identical Mr. Dillon made his appearance, like an *âne entre deux paniers*, with a lady on each arm, both so like himself, that they must have been his mother and sister, though one was short and stout, and the other short and slight."

" That is a good story," remarked Miss Gay, " for he only told us last night, in a disparaging tone, that he could no longer frequent Mrs. Redford's parties."

" Well, for my part," continued Lord Flaxley, laughing heartily, " I thought he played 'your humble servant,' and 'by your leave,' to his hostess, and I must say she gave him the coolest of welcomes. By the bye, shall you dine at Lady Cecilia's the week after next? My father and myself will be there, and I should like to introduce him to you," said he, with an expressive glance at Laura.

She slightly blushed—a good omen, he thought, and informed him they were going into North Wales before the day of the party.

"I hope you will not stay there long, for I shall not be able to find so good an excuse for haunting that neighbourhood, as I have for visiting my constituents, near Sexhurst."

"We shall spend, at least, three months there," answered Laura, coldly.

After musing a few moments, Lord Flaxley rose to go, and with a peculiar smile, asked Miss Owen, if there was any good fly-fishing in that part of North Wales.

"Yes, indeed," she replied, "I believe the fishing in Llanbeddwr Park is excellent."

"But," said Laura, archly, as she shook hands with him, "you surely would not forsake your Parliamentary duties for fly-fishing."

"As for those," he replied, "they are not at all important. I can pair off, and if I lose my seat next election, it is of little consequence to me. I don't owe my distinction to a seat in Parliament, thank heaven!"

"You certainly don't deserve a seat in Parliament, with such notions."

Laura's manner, as she said this, was good-naturedly mocking, and although it gave him some pain, he thought she looked so beautiful and so spirited, that she was just the wife to suit him. Not having birth herself, but possessing beauty, wealth, and talents, he justly considered that her independent notions on the subject, and her ability

and spirit in maintaining them, would be
the surest mode of compelling the respect of
the women, to whom a marriage with him
would introduce her.   As for himself his
views of " birth" had lately undergone some
change ; he now held, that " blood," in the
aristocratic sense, follows the male line,
health and talent the female line.

Pacing briskly along, and revolving these
thoughts, he almost fell into the arms of his
portly parent, as he entered Brooks's.

" Well, my boy," said the Earl of Helston,
" you don't look very gay, this morning."

" I have had a lecture on attention to my
parliamentary duties," replied the young man.

" Bravo ! I am glad to hear that the fair
muse seconds me, though at your age, I
must say, I should not have been quite
so subdued by such a lecture, from such a
quarter."

" We shall not meet them at the Mowbrays."

"They will not meet us, eh?" said the earl, raising his eyebrows, and smiling superciliously, "or, perhaps, they were not invited."

"Yes, I believe they were, but they had previously arranged to leave town before the 22nd."

"Humph! Miss Gay is certainly an original—I should like to see her."

Not that his lordship felt any deep interest in Miss Gay; he had two objections to the match; the chief and most real one, that it was not of his own making—the ostensible one, and the only one, he insisted upon to his son—the lady's plebeian extraction and connections; and in his arguments on this point, he was strenuously supported by his daughter, Lady Mary Flaxley, a girl of Laura's age. The Earl of Helston had, however, evidently begun to modify his disapprobation under the influence of his son's unusual constancy; and partly to teaze his daughter, partly to justify his own want of firmness, he agreed with Lord Flaxley, that " blood " followed the male line only, in the transcendental sense.

In fact, his lordship had no more forcible arguments to use in the matter than empty words, since Lord Flaxley was heir to the earldom and the family estates, and as for threatening him with reducing his allowance, what would that matter to the accepted suitor of Miss Gay? The lady's fortune, too, had real attractions for the earl, and the more he thought of them, the more real they appeared, and the more transcendental and unreal became the claims of blood. Not so, with Lady Mary, who, in common with several brothers and sisters, shared the portion for younger children.

Her ladyship's features, their languid apathy, the graceful stoop, and slender length of her figure, all betokened thoroughly aristocratic birth, breeding, and education. All her ideas were confined to her own class; of all other classes, she had but this general notion, that they formed the masses, from whence the individuals, who served her, either at home, or in the shops, were drawn. Her religious feelings were pontific; she was a Puseyite; for nothing in life had yet shocked her so much as the low churchism of her deceased mother. Moreover, the spirit of equality and the uncompromising reality of the Gospel, alarmed and offended her selfish instincts, making her desire to see these characteristics of Christianity shrouded in ceremonial mystery.

Lord Helston and his son took a turn or two in the park, the latter urging his father to call upon Miss Gay, and the former consenting at last with more amiable condescension than was expected. It was agreed between them that the visit must be made to Miss Owen, his late wife's friend; and the earl entered his house in Carlton Gardens, to inform Lady Mary of his intention. He found her ladyship at home; not like a queen of the olden time, 'sitting in the parlour, eating bread and honey,' but like a most modern maiden, stooping over a piece of gothic embroidery, designed for an altar cloth. Nor did the apartment resemble either a nun's cell, or a mediæval bower; on the contrary, it was quite a modern boudoir, gilded, glazed, and furnished by Gillow.

"Do you know, dear," said his lordship, "wearied by Flaxley's importunities, I have, at length, consented to visit his *bien aimée* to-morrow, and I wish you to accompany me."

"Me, papa!" exclaimed the lady, with unfeigned horror, "surely you cannot be in earnest, my brother must be mad."

"Well, well; perhaps he may be—we must exercise a little charity towards family failings, especially when they manifest themselves on such interesting occasions. We will excuse you a little madness, in love, when a handsome £6000 a-year falls in love with you, eh?"

Lady Mary was neither clever nor brave, so she burst into tears, and left the room, feeling sure that her brother had conquered; that she was a victim to her sex, and to the rights of primogeniture; and the following morning, much against her will, Lady Mary, accompanied her father to Brook Street.

It was on the plea of regard for his wife's memory, that the Earl of Helston called upon Miss Owen, although he had hardly known her by sight during the lifetime of his Countess, and had always manifested a supreme contempt for the canting set among whom his timorous and sickly spouse had taken refuge. Nevertheless, he also ridiculed the turn religious sentiment had taken with his daughter; however, in her case, he considered it such a complete sham, that he used to say, "go on embroidering for ever, my dear, provided you recline sufficiently, I don't think your devotion to the altar will hurt you."

Lord Helston was a vain man, vain of his person, which had been handsome, vain of his family, and its political traditions, vain of his wit, which no one appreciated more highly than himself; and vain of his prudence, which, aided by Lady Helston's delicate health had always kept him within his income. Before his marriage, he had sown but half his wild oats, and since his wife's death, he had resumed that occupation, and now, in a green old age, he was scattering in safe and decent peccadilloes, the remaining half of his measure. It may be imagined then, that it was no less agreeable to him, to inspect a pretty girl, for his son, than it is to a connoisseur in horse-flesh, to inspect a fine animal for his friend.

Precisely at the moment, when ladies are most likely to be found at home, the Earl and Lady Mary drove to Miss Owen's, and asking for that lady, were ushered into her drawing-room.

Laura was so entirely absorbed in the study of business documents, at a writing-table, in the inner room, prior to a call from Mr. Jenkins, that she did not catch the names of Miss Owen's visitors, but perceiving that they were not acquaintances of her own, she continued her occupation; it so happened that she also escaped their observation, being seated in the background, and in a shadier apartment.

Miss Owen expressed a sense of the honour conferred upon her.

"Very glad, indeed, upon my honour, to renew your acquaintance, madam! allow me to present my daughter, Lady Mary. I dare say, you see the likeness to her dear mother. Most extraordinary, I am told."

The young lady looked so utterly apathetic and indifferent, that Miss Owen really perceived no likeness at all, and she replied,

"The features, perhaps, are like, but I don't catch Lady Helston's expression."

"Expression!" ejaculated his lordship, with a smile, and determined to teaze his daughter into complacency, "you are right, madam, no one ever discerned the least expression in my daughter's face. Flaxley, who feels very grateful, I assure you, for the interest you take in him, has all his mother's expression, though in feature, he is said to resemble myself; a great compliment, I take it."

Miss Owen, whose desire to be civil, was equal to anything short of insincerity, was puzzled, and she extricated herself, by declaring she thought the compliment was mutual, and deserved both by father and son.

Lord Helston laughed good-humouredly,

and declared he must send Lord Flaxley to learn equations from Miss Owen.

" My son tells me," added he, " that you have the most charming young friend in the world, staying with you,—one of his constituents, I believe, and he is *au désespoir*, because you are on the point of leaving town. He begged me to get a peep at the fair cause of his madness, that I might become to his ' faults a little blind.' "

(Lord Helston delighted in short quotations.)

The colour came into Miss Owen's cheeks, for greatly as she prized attentions from a man of Lord Helston's degree, she did not like the idea of exposing Laura to what she would consider impertinent and flippant gallantry, and probably resent as such. She was, however, spared a reply by the appearance of Laura herself, who having completed her business, now awaited Mr. Jenkins's call.

She advanced towards the party with a small bundle of papers in her hand, and a very sedate expression of countenance.

His lordship rose to bow; and that he did most respectfully; for he was struck with Laura's beauty, and still more so, by her manner. In fact, Laura had been taught that her eyes were made to see with, and had therefore acquired the habit of scanning the faces of persons presented to her, with the same attention as she bestowed on the title-page of a new book. She mentally concluded Lord Helston to be light reading, and his daughter very blank.

"Lady Mary Flaxley," said his lordship, with a sly glance at that young lady, "has heard so much of Miss Gay from her brother, that she is dying to make her acquaintance. Now, my dear, you can ask Miss Gay whether she prefers embroidering priest's garments like yourself, to knitting scarlet comforters for the Sunday-school children like your poor mother; for I am told that Miss Gay dispenses her favours equally amongst Catholics and Evangelicals, and that she is the benefactress of both Churches. My daughter," said his lordship, turning to Miss Owen, with an assumed air of regret, " is a Puseyite—a sad falling-off is there! However, we are not without hope of conversion, since her sentiments have not as yet passed from the æsthetic to the extatic. They do not go far beyond Gothic embroidery, heavily bound, illluminated prayer-books, and church decorations. Our consolation is the reflection, that the passion for decoration is so common to her age and sex, that it may be as innocently applied, perhaps, to the decoration of the sanctuary made with hands, as to personal adornment."

Laura could not help perceiving the satire, and was sorry for its object, with whom she endeavoured in vain to get up a conversation.

Her efforts were unavailing; the young lady
would not be entertained; and she was
obliged to substitute pity for notice.

"So you are one of my son's chief constituents, Miss Gay. I hope you have no
fault to find with his representation in parliament."

"I told Lord Flaxley," said Laura, with
a smile, "when he came to canvass me,
that talking was more in my line than voting."

"Did you talk him into a proper conception of his duties?"

"I did not attempt it. I believe he received his orders from Mr. Simkins and your
lordship; you know, therefore, far better
than myself how far they were compatible,
and to what extent they have been followed."

"I fear you are not so staunch a Whig as
I had hoped."

"I am not a Whig at all."

"Not a Whig!" exclaimed his lordship,
with a comical expression of surprise, "you

surely don't mean to say you are a Tory ?"

" No," said Laura, " nor a Radical either."

" Thank God! you are not the latter; but what are you then ?"

" A mere looker-on—quite satisfied with things as they are, or rather as they are going to be, and a staunch partisan of honest and capable men."

" Well, but that is exactly what all Whigs profess to be."

" Very well," replied Laura, " they are happy if they can believe so much good of themselves; but, surely, you know that there is a different opinion current respecting your party."

" And pray what is it ?"

" That they are an old family faction, who did good service in their day, and were well paid for it; but that, now, they are devoted to patronage, and not to patriotism."

"That's the unkindest cut of all," re-joined his lordship, rising to go, "I hope, my dear Miss Gay, you don't make mince-meat of my poor boy's political principles; recollect, they are of ancient descent, and he would be nothing without them. Now, my dear," said he, perceiving his daughter was still refractory, and intended only to bow, "shake hands, and don't be so shy."

Lord Helston ordered his coachman to drive in the park: driving through the air s favourable to meditation, especially of a romantic kind. It was some time since either father or daughter had been there, and, perhaps, the young lady had no wish for the drive; however, his lordship did not consult his daughter's inclination, because he was vexed with her, and charmed with Miss Gay.

"What a capital wife to end one's days with," said he to himself, "always cheerful,

I'll be bound; a woman of business; with quite sufficient fortune of her own to portion any family she might be expected to have," and, according to his habit, his enthusiasm vented itself in the following quotation— *sotto voce;* it was one which had frequently haunted his memory of late.

$$\text{ὅπως πρέπει τὰ λεῦκὰ}$$
$$\text{ῥόδοις κρίνα πλακέντα.}$$

"What were you saying, papa," asked Lady Mary, wishing, at length, to break the silence.

"I was merely observing to myself, in Gothic English, that it was better to be an old man's darling, than a young man's snarling."

Lady Mary relapsed into reverie, but ere she slept that night, she had resolved to promote, with all her influence, a marriage between her brother and Miss Gay.

"Well, my lord," said Lord Flaxley to his father, when they met at dinner, "what do you think of Miss Gay? is she not charming?"

"Charming—by Jove! I think she is the loveliest girl I ever saw; a great deal too good for you, my youngster, and were Lord Helston a less honourable man than he is, you would not stand a chance of getting her. However, I'm all for fair play, and I'll give you a couple of months for wooing, and if you don't succeed by the end of that time, I will make Miss Gay, Countess of Helston, myself."

Here was an additional spur to an expeditious courtship; quite unnecessary in Lord Flaxley's present state of feeling,

CHAPTER IV.

IT was now the end of June; moorland
and vale, hedge-row and meadow, were all
bedecked in verdure, buds and blossoms.
The grass was ready for the scythe, the
azalias were mingling their latest perfume
with the sweet scent of the first mignionette,
and the first roses of summer. Strawberries
were ripening, bees were busy—the lime tree
was about to flower—the paths were swept,
the lawn fresh mown; and the faithful genius
of the Dell was standing at the gate, awaiting

the arrival of the beloved mistress, whom he had known from the day of her birth.

He is, indeed, a paragon, and deserves far more than an episode to celebrate his worth; but neither to fame nor fortune did he ever look for inducements to tread the path of duty.

Now, he stands bareheaded, leaning on the wicket of the lodge garden, in the midst of sweetbriar, double stocks, ladslove and wallflowers, clad in blue plush and mulberry cloth (for on gala days, it was his pride to wear the Gay livery,) while over his furrowed face and cheeks, firm and rosy as the far-famed nectarines of the Dell, plays a bright smile, whose pure and simple source, a child well might envy.

He is a pensioner, and has been such these four years, yet no four years of his hard working life have been more zealously devoted to faithful service than these last. Four and twenty years ago, old John had charge of the shrubberies and plantations at

Sexhurst, and his zeal and trust-worthiness there having attracted Mr. Gay's notice, he made him a sort of bailiff. When the Rev. Watkyn Owen died, he was transferred to the Dell, there to act as coachman and chief manager for the widow, his eldest son, in whose education Mr. Gay had always taken an interest, being made bailiff at Sexhurst..

A commodious and comfortable lodge was built for old John at the Dell, but he and his only daughter had not long inhabited it, when he met with an accident, which nearly cost him his life. One fine morning, Maria had gone to help to wash at the Dell, and the old man, as usual, on such occasions, rose early too, to clean and sweep his small apartment, and to prepare breakfast. It struck him that the small window of his scullery might be cleaner, and he was rubbing it, when the glass broke, and entered the palm of his right hand. Inflammation ensued, mortification took place, and for many days he lay in considerable danger, and, at last, the first and second fingers were amputated. Laura, Mrs. Owen, and Maria vied with each other as tender nurses; and, on his recovery, Mr. Gay bought him an annuity equal to his wages, telling him that, in future, he would not be expected to work, but that if he kept an eye over gardeners, grooms, and labourers, this liberality would be amply requited. Old John, however, thought differently, for to the most scrupulous overseeing, he added the occupation of cultivating the fruit, and the rose trees, and surely no roses, and no peaches and nectarines could surpass those he produced.

A few minutes, and carriage wheels were heard—the gate was flung open, and the carriage stopped for a moment. The mutilated hand of the old man was shaken by Laura, with a "Dear old John, how well

you are looking," and " God bless you, Miss
Laura, you be no worse this time for
Lunnun air."

Maria was up at the house; the servants
had arrived, and all was fresh and clean, as
only a country-house can be. The sweetest of
roses, the finest of strawberries, the freshest
of eggs, and the clearest of honey, were served
to the travellers; and even Miss Owen acknowledged, that the country was preferable
to the town in summer time.

" How quiet it is," she said, " how fragrant
and how beautiful. Yet, dear Laura, it must
recall to you the sad event of last year, and
such regrets must mingle with the pleasures of
this delightful welcome."

" Regrets may become dear, and pleasant to
think upon, when they recall the love and goodness of our earliest friends, especially, when the
mourner is not friendless; and thanks to you,
dear Miss Owen, I have long ceased to be
so."

Miss Owen did not reply. She only sighed.

"Why do you sigh?"

"I ought not to repine, since your affection, Laura, has given me a new life, never, I hope to give place again to the old one; but, dearest girl, I cannot help dreading the time, when another, more worthy of your love, more capable of making you happy, will naturally take my place, and I shall cease to be of any importance to you and Lord Flaxley."

"That will never be," replied Laura, gaily, "in the first place, Lord Flaxley is too volatile and too aristocratic in his notions to marry, or to suit me, and in the second," she continued, in a lower and more serious tone, "I have long loved another, to whom it is improbable I shall ever be united. Can you suppose me capable," she added, in a voice of cheerful reproach, "of forsaking one who has been so kind a friend to me in my need, as yourself. No, indeed, whoever marries Laura Gay, must also take for better and for worse, her excellent friend and companion, Miss Owen."

Miss Owen's apprehensions were relieved, and now she became excessively curious to know, who had so long possessed our heroine's heart. She was, however, obliged to rest in doubt, for Laura was not inclined to make any further confession, and *she* could think of no probable person, faithless or rejected.

The following morning was one of pleasureable business. Every chamber, and every nook of house and grounds were visited. Laura's pretty half-bred Arabian galloway received his mistress's caresses, and her father's stout cob was patted too. The collection of new books they had bought in town, and Miss Owen's new fancy-work patterns, were all conveniently placed for use. The presents were laid out for bestowal. Pruning knives, and budding knives of the best construction for old John, with a sensible book or two, gowns, shawls, scissors, and prize books for servants and school-children; and, lastly, what had afforded the greatest pleasure in selection, a large box of things for the parsonage, containing toys for all ages, books, and fancy work.

The servants were in a bustle of enjoyment, and, in the midst of it all, in came the good parson and his sweet little wife, delighted to have Miss Gay near them again. Well might they be so; for she was a neighbour, with whom, frank-hearted people like themselves could live on terms of perfect confidence.

"You have played the absentee far too long, my dear Miss Gay," said Mr. Gardiner. "I hope now, you will spend some time with us."

"We intend doing so," said Laura, glancing at Miss Owen. "Now, tell me, what changes have occurred in the neighbourhood since last autumn. Not many, I dare say," she concluded with a smile.

"Indeed you are mistaken. A very great, and not altogether a beneficial change, I regret to say, is coming over our hitherto secluded district. Perhaps you recollect, that a couple of years ago, Mr. Owen's agent began to work some slate quarries on the hill-side, between the church, and Llanbeddwr Park. Well, these quarries have assumed rather an extensive development, and no provision of dwellings having been made for the workmen, who receive higher wages than the peasantry around, and are unsettled in their habits, they frequent our hamlet to the detriment of its fair fame and morals."

Laura was much surprised, for she had never heard of the quarries, until Mr. Brocklebank asked her about them: and then she had not believed in their existence.

"What a shame," exclaimed Miss Owen,

"to spoil our picturesque mountain sides, with horrid quarries, and the din of blasting, and quarrymen, just to increase the wealth of one man, who came unexpectedly into an estate, which was good enough to satisfy my father."

Mr. Gardiner agreed with her.

"I think," objected Laura, "we have no right to blame Mr. Owen, for making the most of his property, nor should we regret, that our noble mountain is compelled to yield forth its treasures, for the use of man; what, under Heaven, is a more cheerful sight, than a busy and virtuous community, producing by its toil and labour, comforts that are enjoyed elsewhere. Do not let us set up poetry and the picturesque, as idols of our fancy above human weal and well doing."

Mr. Gardiner was thoughtful; at last, he said, "you are right, in the main, Miss Gay, but what troubles me in the present

case, is, that the new sprung industry is
so irregular in its habits. If the men
had houses, they would marry, and lead
more respectable lives, and would become
accessible to moral and religious influences;
as it is, they toil, and spend the fruits
of their toil in criminal indulgences."

"Have you represented this to Mr.
Owen, or his agent?"

"Yes. But the former leaves all his
business to the latter, who, in his turn, declares, that he is content to work the
quarries faithfully, and that he has neither
the capital at his disposal, or the time
to attend to more."

"Well then," exclaimed Laura, energeti-
cally, "you and I will do it — *we* see the
evil, and it is our business to remedy it.
You know I have a tract of woodland, a
little above the new national schools; there
I will build a row of good cottages, and we
will hive our bees in the parish enclosure."

It was at once agreed, that Miss Gay should drive to the spot that evening, there to meet Mr. Gardiner and old John, for the purpose of surveying the ground, and considering its sanitory capabilities.

Laura wrote off to Mr. Simkins for plans of cottage buildings, and, in return, she received from that worthy employer of men, a large bundle of designs, and measurements, with remarks, and estimates, superadded by Mr. Peter Simkins, the son, who offered to come over, at a day's notice, if he could be of the slightest assistance to Miss Gay. Miss Owen suggested that it would give him and his eldest sister, much pleasure to visit at the Dell; accordingly, they were invited to spend a few days—an invitation which they accepted with alacrity.

Activity and cheerfulness had fairly taken possession of the Dell, and of Llanbeddwr hamlet. Old John summoned the steadiest masons and labourers of the country-side;

the services of a good builder from Glynsbrynn, and a clever practical surveyor were
engaged to make the most complete arrangements for a proper supply of water and
drainage. Laura and Mr. Gardiner kept a
watchful eye over all; Mr. Peter Simkins
enforced economy, convenience, and substantial work; whilst old John maintained so
wary a supervision, that not an item of the
contract could be shirked.

The month of July passed merrily enough.
Miss Simkins and Miss Owen drove out,
walked out, and chatted together. They
visited the poor, discussed cottage house-
keeping, recipes for preserving fruits and
turning lettuce stalks into West India ginger.
They watched the bees, and filled the flower
vases. Laura scoured the country on her
galloway, frequently riding to the quarries,
escorted by Mr. Gardiner, on her father's cob,
and there learning from the agent the difference between princesses, duchesses, coun-

tesses, and ladies' slates—titles far more characteristic of the quality of slates, than they are of the quality of the women who likewise bear them. She made the acquaintance of some of the quarry lads, and had the satisfaction of learning that, with an eye to her cottages, several of them were keeping company with respectable young women. At the end of the month, the foundations were rising above the ground; Mr. Peter Simkins and his sister had returned to Littleborough, and preparation was being made at the Dell to receive the Brocklebanks, and the Mowbrays, whilst Mr. and Mrs. Owen, and a distinguished party were also expected at the Hall. So, at least, it was stated in the " Glynsbrynn Farmer's Advertiser."

In the course of a few days, the Owens and the Brocklebanks arrived by the same train from town. They met, to Mrs. Owen's great surprise, on the Glynsbrynn platform, and after exchanging civilities, Mr. Owen—

who often felt embarrassed on such occasions
—was commencing a speech, that must have
concluded with an invitation to spend a few
days at Llanbeddwr Hall, but feeling the
muscle of his arm forcibly pressed by his wife's
forefinger, he changed his profession of hospitality into hopes, that they should have the
pleasure of seeing Mr. Mrs. and Miss
Brocklebank to lunch at an early day.

Mr. and Mrs. Brocklebank related this
little incident with good-humoured ridicule,
on arriving at the Dell, where they found a
thoroughly hearty welcome from both ladies.
It seemed, indeed, to Miss Owen, who up
to the time of her residence with Laura, had
never been treated with respect by the world,
that Laura Gay carried with her an atmosphere of charity and unworldliness, which
made those who met, under her auspices,
friends, in spite of themselves, their rank,
or their wealth.

Mrs. Brocklebank was worthy of her

husband.   She was fresh and comely, forty-five, with the proper embonpoint—matronly, amiable, independent and good-hearted.   The word 'solid' expressed not her figure only, but her character, intellectual and moral. All her ideas were solid, formed on substantial realities,—of fancy, she had not a jot,—a flower was a flower, a landscape was, hill, vale, woodland and water, but utterly undecked with any sentimental association. High principle was the genius of her soul, the object of all her enthusiasm.   She liked, in her own words, those who know that wrong is wrong, and right is right.   It follows, therefore, that she loved her husband, that she liked Laura Gay and Miss Owen, and that she entertained no such feeling towards such people as Mrs. Owen and Mr. Dillon.   They all sat down to dinner, at a sociable round table, and conversation was general and constant.

" Well, Miss Gay, have you discovered any slate quarries ?" asked Mr. Brocklebank.

"Yes, indeed, and I am ashamed that I asserted their non-existence so positively. It seems they have been worked two years, and latterly with considerable success. In fact, there are so many labourers employed, in them, that I have begun to build cottages for them."

"Let me advise you to beware of bricks and mortar."

"Oh! I thought those were only dangerous, in the shape of porticoes, lodges, conservatories, fanciful school-houses, and the like."

"If you aim at being the veritable Lady Bountiful, or the tasty foundress of a village, bricks and mortar may assume a dangerous form in the shape of châlets, hermitages, Elizabethan cottages, and so forth—far less comfortable in reality for poor people than substantial square buildings."

"Mine," said Laura, "are substantial, nearly square, and in a row; but you shall see them, or rather their foundations, to-morrow."

"Don't you think we had better lunch at Llanbeddwr Hall to-morrow? There's nothing like striking while the iron is hot," suggested Mr. Brocklebank, with a comical smile at Laura.

"You had better see the quarries first, I think, my dear," observed Mrs. Brockle-bank, whose maxim in life had always been "business first and pleasure afterwards."

"Madame's pride, you see, Miss Gay, will not brook inhospitable friendship in the country; but my dear," turning to his wife, "there are great excuses to be made for people like the Owens—in fact, the best of all excuses, ignorance; and if my fair matron had been like your humble servant, a man of business, she would have learned that to others, we must sometimes mete a less rigid rule than absolute right. These sort of people are like children; they live in daydreams and fancies. They come to me to assist in making them rich; they forget I have other friends to serve, and a sacred trust to fulfil. They fancy their quarries, their lands, and themselves occupy as large a place in my mind, as in their own. Besides wealth, they covet a high position in society, which they estimate according to a standard somewhat out of date in this changing world. Their only criteria are, birth, a title, a park, and a Hall. They have yet to learn the importance of that power which we know and possess; they have little acquaintance with real life, and they don't know that, he who can command education, assume government, give employment, and bestow wealth, is a real lord among men."

"I despise persons," rejoined his lady, "who hesitate to invite you to meet those who cannot do them a pennyworth of good, at the very time that they are begging you to put thousands into their pockets."

"No, no, my dear, we will not despise them; we will only laugh at them, lunch with them, and recollect that they are of the time-honoured genus—country gentleman."

"No," said Laura, "not a fair sample of the genus. It is far more respectable. This is only a species of it."

"For my part," rejoined Mrs. Brockle-bank, "I cannot like people who are deficient in the sentiment of common honesty."

"Those sentiments cannot exist without common sense, like your own, my dear, and I am sure you are too good to condemn any one who is not gifted with that."

"I hear," remarked Miss Owen to Laura, "that Lord and Lady Huntley, and the Dowager, are coming to the Hall to-morrow."

"Indeed? then we certainly will go to lunch there," said Laura, "even you, Mrs. Brocklebank will like Lord Huntley, for he is a *raal* gentleman, every inch of him, and *no* mistake, although he is Mrs. Owen's eldest brother."

It was finally agreed, that the whole party should go to see the cottages in the morning, and should call at the Parsonage, to ask the Gardiners to dine at the Dell; and that the next day Mr. Brocklebank and Laura should ride over the moors, to inspect the quarries; and, probably, the day after, weather permitting, drive through Llanbeddwr woods and Park, to lunch at the Hall. The next morning was overcast and sunny by turns, and the whole party at the Dell, decided upon walking to the hamlet, and having the carriage come for them to the Parsonage, to take home those who were not equal to returning on foot, or in case of rain to convey them all.

The cottages were duly surveyed, and obtained both Mr. and Mrs. Brocklebank's approval. The latter suggested a few additional conveniencies, and alterations, but her husband begged to remind her, that any alterations would impair the consistency of the plan, and that she, being so great a stickler for consistency, could not be so inconsistent as to persist in her suggestions. The good lady smiled, and admitted that she thought Miss Gay had better keep to the original plans, without heeding the remarks of critics.

"The only fault I have to find," pursued Mr. Brocklebank, "is, that the houses are too good; you will have to settle in one of them yourself, to teach the poor people how to enjoy all the comforts you are providing for them."

"Where there's a will, there's a way, Sir," remarked old John, who was standing by unobserved; the fact was, the faithful old fellow recognized one of his late master's sort in Mr. Brocklebank.

"Certainly, and that being the case, Miss Gay is sure to have her way, I suppose?"

"I should reckon so, Sir, seeing as she's our master's daughter, as was."

"So my veteran, you are one of Mr. Gay's old servants."

"That he is!" said Laura, "and one of my best friends to boot."

"And how long have you lived in the family?"

"Why, Sir, I can't say as I can just tell all at once like, but let's see," putting the third finger of his right hand upon his lips in token of abstraction: "it's strange how one's memory wears out, Sir, but how old is Miss Laura, Sir? for I came full two years afore she was born."

"There, Miss Laura!" exclaimed Mr. Brocklebank, "what say you to this good man's chronology? How do you like the idea of making your birth an epoch?"

Laura laughed, and at once confessed her age, after which, old John computed that he had been some little above twenty-four years in the family. At this moment, they were joined by Mr. Gardiner, and introductions passed round.

"We have been admiring Miss Gay's cottages," said Mrs. Brocklebank, to whose side the reverend gentleman attached himself, seemingly by sympathy with straightforwardness.

"Perhaps, *you* may not have so much reason for admiring them," observed Mr. Brocklebank, "since their occupants, a rough set, I should fear, will be your neighbours, and add greatly to your parish labours."

"My parish is a small one, and 1 shall be glad to have it increased."

"If you approve of it," said Laura, "I shall be very happy to support a Scripture reader, whenever you require assistance."

"That is exactly the sort of assistance I should like, in case I felt myself unequal to the population of the parish."

"Ah, ah! my good Sir: you will never hold a Bishoprick, I fear," remarked Mr. Brocklebank.

"I have no wish to do so," replied Mr. Gardiner, with a frank, cheerful smile. "The Episcopal chair is little suited to the nature of one, whose *vocation*, no less than his profession, is the care of souls. But I am forgetting my errand—Mrs. Gardiner told me you were here, and bade me ask you to give her a call."

"We came with that intention," replied Miss Owen, "and to ask you to dine with us to-day."

The invitations were both accepted, and as they approached the parsonage—a simple erection, built with regard to the comfort and health of its inmates, rather than for appearance, they could not help admiring its picturesque situation, the perfect cultivation of its little garden, and the fruitfulness of the orchard.

"There," said Mr. Gardiner, pointing to a well grown blooming boy and girl, who were budding roses, " are our chief gardeners; it is a rule of my wife's to make the children useful from the earliest age; you see the profit of it, in the state of our garden, and in the healthy appearance of the children. We find the advantage of it, in habits of order and cheerfulness during study, and of consideration towards those who surround them."

Nothing could be plainer than the furniture of the parsonage, and the dress of Mrs. Gardiner, and her children; yet, as nothing could be neater and cleaner, this plainness was rather *distingué* and agreeable than otherwise. There was the same unalloyed simplicity in their manners and conversation—no inuendo, or insinuation; the quizzing smile, and the furtive glance were all unknown among them. Not that they were ignorant of the world, but that their hearts were kept pure and unspotted from it.

After repeating the invitation to dinner, to Mrs. Gardiner, Mr. Gardiner, Laura, and Miss Brocklebank joined the young rose-budders in the garden. This was a signal to three little urchins in the orchard for a game at romps; and presently, the whole village echoed with peals of merry laughter from the parsonage grounds.

While, in the midst of their sport, the Honourable Mrs. Owen, as her servant loudly proclaimed her, drove up to the door. She had not yet laid aside her air of London languor.

"How do, my dear," said she to Frank Gardiner. "Is mamma at home?"

She had by her side a little boy of four years old, who looked quite afraid of the congregation of little Gardiners, and clung to his mother.

"Poor child! he is so sensitive among strangers, especially country children," she exclaimed affectedly, as she entered the house with Miss Gay.

No one seemed very glad to see her, but every one was civil; and the Dell party soon rose to take leave.

" My dear Miss Gay," said Mrs. Owen, in a tone which might have accompanied the tooth-ache, so plaintive was it, " perhaps you will spare me the unnecessary fatigue of a drive to the Dell this morning. I intended calling there; but since I have had the good fortune to meet you, will you allow me to hope that you will bring your guests to lunch with us to-morrow. My brother and his wife, Lord and Lady Huntley (for the benefit of the Brocklebanks), and my mother will be with us, and perhaps one or two others. I hope Mr. and Mrs. Brocklebank and their daughter will do us the honour of coming," looking with a languid droop of the head in their direction.

" I think," said Mrs. Brocklebank, whose dislike of affectation was getting the better of her politeness, " we have other engagements."

"No, my dear," replied her husband, "I think we may combine our plans for to-morrow very well indeed, with luncheon at the Hall."

"We had better accept Mrs. Owen's invitation," interposed Laura; "because I have received a note this morning from Lady Cecilia Mowbray, in which they propose to be with us about lunch-time, the day after to-morrow."

This settled the question, and threw Mrs. Owen into a state of great surprise. "Did that queer girl, Laura Gay, think of mixing up classes in such an extraordinary way, as to have the Mowbrays, and the Brocklebanks altogether in her house at the same time," thought she to herself.

When they had left, she asked Mr. Gardiner, "how long those people—I really can't quite recollect their name—are staying at the Dell?"

"About a week," he replied, "do you

know them?   They are very agreeable, intelligent people."

"I dare say they are good enough in their way," she vouchsafed to say, just as though the ways of being good, differed for each human being.

Mr. Gardiner flattered no foibles even in his principal parishioners; he, therefore, observed:

"We are all subject to the same moral and physical laws, and the light of one common revelation has been bestowed upon all Christians; goodness, gentleness, and intelligence can only be measured by a standard common to all."

Mrs. Owen did not like the tone of what he said, and although she could not quite understand it, she thought it must be fallacious; and feeling very much inclined towards the High Church, she choose to consider Mr. Gardiner very low indeed. Nevertheless, out of regard to her brother, she invited Mr. Gardiner and his lady to lunch at the Hall the next day.

"Poor little Harry," said she, kissing her child, as soon as the horse's heads were turned towards home, "I don't wonder at his being frightened by those coarse, vulgar children; they are not like the little Melvilles he used to play with in the park, are they, dear? did he not see what brown hands they had, and what short, cropped hair. I dare say they have no nice gloves to put on, poor things! and no kind nurse to make them pretty curls like these," added she, winding one of Harry's glossy ringlets round her finger.

Thus did this silly mother instil the first indelible prejudices of wealth, birth, and effeminacy, into the tender mind of her little son. What kind of morality in after life could be expected to combine with this sort of early education.

.

CHAPTER V.

NOTHING could exceed the beauty of the weather the following morning. Light fleecy clouds were calmly sailing through a sky of the deepest blue, dappling the most enchanting shade and shine over the valley and hill sides; the temperature of the air was exhilirating, although it promised to become hot towards noon. However, the road to the quarries lay on the shady side of the hill, and from the quarries to Llanbeddwr Hall, through woods all the way, if the equestrians chose to make a circuit of two miles. Allowing, therefore, for the ascent to the quarries, half an

hour spent there, and the round, Mr. Brocklebank and Miss Gay set off an hour and a
half earlier than the carriage party.

As they rode along, Mr Brocklebank
admired, by turns, the changing scene,
Laura's bright bay galloway, her costume,
her *entourage* at the Dell, her friends at the
Parsonage, and last, not least, her faithful
servitor, old John.

He was in a state of great delight, by no
means common to a man of his age, for alas!
there are few among us, who retain to the
last, the youthful zest for beauty, virtue and
truth. But Mr. Brocklebank was a man of
genial intellect, his enjoyment of nature and
character was great, and he possessed, in a
high degree, that experience of life, and that
keen perception, which enables one to " point
a moral, or adorn a tale."

His conversation did not flag throughout
the ride. He entertained Laura with a
number of anecdotes, illustrative of railway

roguery, the chicanery of joint stock speculations, and contractor's dodges.

"At present," said he, "the railway board on which I sit, is tolerably honest, but its chances of continuing so, are not very hopeful. It is so much the interest of underlings to have King Log for their master, and a divided government at the head of affairs, that they will move heaven and earth to introduce dummies to fill up any vacancy which occurs in the Direction."

"At the present moment, they are doing all in their power to bring Mr. Redford amongst us, although he is a man without an atom of fixed principle, and with a sarcastic spirit, enough to turn any discussion sour, and to set us all by the ears. As for myself, I have no business of my own to attend to, and I have the taste for commercial pursuits sufficiently strong to make it an object to me to continue a Director, at a nominal remuneration."

This was neither Cicero, Dante, nor Shakespeare, but it was extremely instructive to Laura Gay, and she felt herself no less invigorated by the spirit of energetic uprightness, which characterized her companion, than by the mountain air and the exercise they were enjoying, and she might well have been held up by strong-minded friends, as a model to love-lorn damsels.

Nevertheless, Charles Thornton was rarely absent from her heart; after Platonic fashion, she had divided him into two natures: the one full of noble impulse and generous instincts manifested in his pamphlet, his speeches, and his political career; the other of common kind, fitted for the salon, and the club, and subject to the passions and interests of worldly existence. The former was still the ideal of her loving fancy: for the latter, she was endeavouring to cultivate indifference.

As they approached the quarries,

they were not a little surprised to meet
old John. "The old fellow is your
shadow," remarked Mr. Brocklebank.

"Not generally," replied Laura. "We
are still on my land, and I have no doubt,
that my interest in some form or other
brings him hither."

"Well, John," said she, "it is an unexpected pleasure to meet you here."

"I doubt, raly ma'am, whether you'll
say so, when you know as I've nothing but
suspicions to tell you."

"You have come rather a long way to
communicate them, and pray whom do they
concern?"

"Them quarries, there, as is getting precious
close up against us, and one of our mason's
down yon, said summut, as how his brother
as overlooks the quarries, said as they'd be
a delving under us, afore long, and that's
what I call deceteful, and I'd like to stop it
with your leave, Miss."

"That is to say, my sagacious friend, you would like to put a stop to it, before it becomes a question for the lawyers."

"Yes, Sir, and I thought as you'd be like enough to put Miss Gay into a good way, Sir."

"The question for Miss Gay to consider is, whether a vein of slate runs into her property sufficiently valuable to pay the working, and such watching as would effectually prevent any infringement of her rights."

Old John remarked, " that when Mr. Gay bought that tract of moorland, he had said, 'it had cost him an old song, but he had reason to think, some time or other it would well repay the purchase.'"

"No doubt, then, he thought it contained mineral treasures."

The quarries were examined, and it seemed both to Laura and her companion, that the depth of the slate strata increased as they approached her property. It was, therefore, agreed, that Mr. Brocklebank should write

to a good practical geologist and land surveyor, to come and make such an examina-
tion of the ground as would enable Miss Gay
to decide, whether she would commence
quarrying slate. At the same time, he laugh-
ingly said, " he may send me a report of the
cost of making a line of railway to the quarries,
and the probable return the traffic would yield;
for he has already been employed on several
railways, and is a very sagacious fellow."

They had a delightful galop through the
woods, and when they reached the Hall, they
found they were at least twenty minutes in
advance of their own party, and a little
earlier than was expected.

The servant who received them, said that
Mr. and Mrs. Owen, with most of their
friends, had sauntered out, some ten minutes
before towards the grotto—a cool, sequestered
spot, about five minutes' walk from the house.
Laura decided to go in, and Mr. Brocklebank to find the grotto, with the help of

a garden boy, who was called to conduct him.

Laura passed through the spacious and luxuriously-furnished drawing-room to Mrs. Owen's boudoir, where at times like these, when the house was full of company, she was sure of finding some rare and costly plant, and a book or two, *très à-la-mode.*

The carpet was Axminster, and Laura's step was noiseless. The first objects that arrested her attention, on entering the boudoir, were, the picture of Rome, which had so potently attracted and moved her at the Exhibition, hanging over the mantle-piece, and a gentleman gazing upon it with intense interest. He was Charles Thornton. She could not mistake the figure, or the head, though she did not catch a glimpse of his face.

Fortunately for Laura Gay, her entrance had not disturbed his contemplations; for, in the excessive flutter of her spirits, she felt incapable even of retreat. She leaned against a marble slab standing exactly behind her, and after considerable effort, succeeded in regaining her composure. Luckily, the business-like conversation, and her ride, came in aid of all those mental and moral pre- parations with which she fancied she had so successfully strengthened herself, since her last rencontre with Charles Thornton at the Royal Academy. Nor would she allow herself to think that he was looking at that picture with the same kind of interest she had felt.

At last, he turned round, with something between a sigh and a stretch, in the midst of which he was arrested by the apparition of Laura Gay, wearing the very costume in which he had last beheld her at Rome, ex- cepting, perhaps, that the Brazilian hat and white feather she now wore, gave her a more fairy-like aspect.

Could it really be Laura? The colour mounted to his temples, as he gazed in ardent, breathless bewilderment. She cast down her eyes, while the eloquent blood in her cheeks would have spoken volumes to one less surprised and embarrassed than was Charles Thornton at that moment.

"Good Heavens!" at last he exclaimed in a voice of great agitation, leaning back against the mantle piece, "how—what brought you here?"

At that moment, he remembered that Lord Flaxley was there also, and as Laura looked up, his countenance changed, assuming an expression of rigid self-control.

Laura had been aware of his first emotion, but she resolved to practice no self-delusion, and his affected coolness assisting her now, she replied with forced calmness.

"I had no idea of finding you here, when I entered the house. I did not even know that you were acquainted with the Owens, when I accepted the invitation to meet some friends at lunch."

Thornton's emotion was great—pique, jealousy, sudden disappointment and renewed grief, were all struggling with affection for the mastery.

He answered Laura's speech, by a low bow, which reminded her of the Flower Show.

At last, he said, in a serious melancholy voice, pointing, at the same time to the Roman landscape, " are you then willing to forget all that passed there?"

Laura's heart beat fast, the tears were ready to fall; she sought to escape, and crossing the room to an open door, leading through the conservatory into the garden, she replied with as much firmness as she could muster:

" It is best to forget."

Thornton was startled by her sudden departure, and feeling that a favourable moment was not to be lost for a complete explanation, he followed her through the conservatory; but what was his dismay and mortification, to see her immediately meet the whole party, now returning to the house; foremost amongst whom was Lord Flaxley.

His lordship's delight at meeting her was evident to all.

Thornton would have given worlds to be able to see her face at that moment, but he could judge by the significant smile, and the pleasure expressed on the countenances of the beholders, that hers, too, was beaming with pleasure.

He returned to the boudoir, with heavy heart, and took up a new book of sentimental philosophy, lying on the table; not to dive deep into its contents, but to dive deep into meditation respecting Laura Gay's present to feelings.

He could not conceal from himself, that on this occasion, her agitation was considerably less than before, although she must have perceived how great was his own; still, her countenance had betrayed emotion;

her last words were certainly uttered in a
fluttered manner, and she had feared to
prolong the *téte-à-téte*.   He saw clearly how
it was; reason, that dangerous thing in women, and a will, accustomed to constant exercise, were on the side of her offended pride,
and she would not forgive him, that hasty,
that fatal day at the Flower Show.   No, she
would rather sacrifice the natural feelings of
her heart, than pardon such an offence
against her dignity.   Perhaps now, too, she
had resolved to call in ambition to her aid.
He could not doubt that Lord Flaxley had
accepted the Owens invitation for no other
purpose, than to be near Laura, and he feared
she might have given some encouragement to
his attentions.

It was not long ere his reveries were
interrupted by the sound of merry voices;
some of them quite unknown to his ear,
for the drawing-room was now full of
the lunch party, all of whom had arrived.

He heard Lord Flaxley say to Mrs. Owen :

" Where is Thornton ? What a solitary bird he is. I want to present him to Miss Gay," to which Miss Gay replied :

" He is already an acquaintance of mine. I saw him just now in the boudoir."

Thornton rose, sighing deeply, and was on the point of putting down his book, when Lord Flaxley entered, and taking it up, opened it at a chapter, entitled, " The soul's first glimpse."

" Upon my soul, Thornton, how can you read such trash, when your soul can get glimpses to your heart's content, among all the bright eyes yonder. Come along, you will learn more there, in ten minutes, about the human soul, than any book would teach you in a month. Come, I want to hear you talk to Miss Gay ; she is something in your own line, only a devilish deal more fascinating."

Thornton advanced into the drawing-room, with so very solemn an air, that Lord Flaxley regarded him with surprise, not knowing whether to consider him shy or proud. He could not succeed in getting up a conversation between his lady-love and his much-admired friend, so he was fain to confine his attentions to the former, concluding, in his own mind, that there was a conscious rivalry of talent between them, which kept them apart. His memory reverted to the only instance of the kind, with which it was furnished; that of Talleyrand and Madame de Staël, both of whom his father had once known, and still gloried to talk about, and he flattered himself that his own affections were fixed on a second Corinne.

Mrs. Owen's satisfaction was complete, when her guests sat down to the stylish lunch prepared for them, and she felt rewarded by the complimentary ideas, which she felt sure, each guest entertained of her elegant hospitality, and high breeding, and of the charity and good nature that had induced her to invite the Brocklebanks and the Gardiners.

How far, anything beyond the actual enjoyment of good cheer, and of each other's conversation, occupied their thoughts, it is impossible to say, but from what we know of the naturally various characters assembled round her table, it is probable that the sum of their admiration, fell short of Mrs. Owen's estimate.

However, she was satisfied, and it is well that satisfaction should follow good intentions, even when performed by persons of inferior merit. We do not mean to say, that most of those present were not enjoying themselves, indeed, it was evident that with two exceptions, (and even they would not have wished themselves away), every one was gratified.

Dowager Lady Huntley was proud to see her daughter at the head of such a table, and was pleased with everybody, because she was sure they agreed with her, that her dear child graced the position. Lord Huntley was pleased, because he thought his precious wife looked as charming as any of the pretty women there, and because he liked Mr. Gardiner and Miss Gay, and thought he should like the Brocklebanks. In fact, it was in Lord Huntley's nature to be easily pleased.

The Brocklebanks were pleased with their visit into Wales, and with the fine weather; Mr. Brocklebank was pleased to have so full a page of human nature spread out before him. He liked Charles Thornton, Laura, the Gardiners, Miss Owen, and Lord Huntley; and he was disposed to think well of Lord Flaxley, for Laura's sake—perhaps, over-hastily concluding that something like an engagement subsisted between them. Miss Brocklebank was pleased to be at table (albeit a most sensible and cultivated young person) with real lords and ladies, and to find herself seated next to Mr. Thornton, who, besides being a very handsome man, according to her taste, was one whom she had always heard mentioned with respect.

Miss Owen was pleased to inform Mrs. Brocklebank and her daughter, that her infancy and youth had been passed amid the splendour of Llanbeddwr Hall, whilst the present owner had only come into its possession by the accident, as it were, of one brother's death, and the other's childlessness. However, her esteem for Lord Huntley was so great, that she waxed daily more indulgent towards his sister.

As for Lord Flaxley, having inherited his full share of the family vanity with his ancient descent, he was quite enchanted to find himself the chief person there, in the midst of beauty, talent, and worth, and the cavalier of by far the handsomest, cleverest, and sweetest woman in the room. The elevation of his spirits, and his proximity to herself, were far from agreeable to Laura; she would rather have found herself near a quieter neighbour, where she might have bestowed more time in reflecting on what had passed in the boudoir, and in noting upon Charles Thornton's countenance, symptoms of that change of feeling which, she supposed, made him now desirous of liberation from the quasi-engagement into which he had thoughtlessly fallen at Rome. Moreover, notwithstanding her intention of releasing him, whenever a convenient opportunity should offer; and notwithstanding her conviction of his indifference, she was much mortified that *he* should be a witness of Lord Flaxley's attentions. What could be more inopportune?—and to make matters worse, Charles Thornton sat on the opposite side of the table; and though too far to hear what passed between them, he was able to observe Laura's uneasiness, and her blushes, all of which he did observe and interpret in a way very tormenting to himself: to cover his misery, he wore an air of attention to pretty Miss Brocklebank, which Laura remarked every time she could look in their direction, and which she took to mean an open repudiation of the possibility of his loving herself any longer.

Mrs. Brocklebank sat exactly opposite to Lord Flaxley, who proposed to make a third in the ride homewards towards the Dell. Every one agreed that nobody could think of returning in the heat of the day, and that it would be much better to saunter about the shrubberies, to inspect the lake, the grotto, and the pinetum, and to defer leaving till near five o'clock, when the glow of the noon-day sun would have somewhat abated.

As they rose from lunch, Dowager Lady Huntley proposed that the dear children should come down into the drawing-room.

"It is quite unfair," said she, "that nurse should always keep those lovely little angels to herself. What used they to call Harry in Rome, my love?

" Il bambinetto; and Datteschi was always coaxing us to let him have him for a model for a Sagra Famiglia he had engaged to paint for the King of Bavaria."

The gentlemen, however, feeling no curiosity to see il bambinetto, and the later bambinetti, adjourned to the stables, by Mr. Owen's invitation. Lord Flaxley was inclined to be civil to Mr. Brocklebank, first, because he looked like a man whose good opinion was worth having; secondly, because he was a friend of Miss Gay's; thirdly, because his wife was well-looking, and his daughter very pretty and elegant; and, lastly, because all these good reasons for civility were crowned by the halo of wealth. They walked together from the stables; and Mr. Brocklebank remarked to Lord Flaxley, that Lord Huntley was a much more favourable specimen of his class than his sister, Mrs. Owen.

" Yes, something due to sex—something to his cloth," replied his lordship, knocking the ash, from the point of his cigar, " but after all, Huntley is only a poor Viscount ; and there is not much in such a position, you know, to support pride."

A significant smile, which Lord Flaxley did not see, played upon Mr. Brocklebank's face, as he animadverted, inwardly, on the fine distinctions vanity draws for us, to raise us above those of our fellows, who do not possess exactly the same advantages as ourselves.

The bambino and bambinetti, meanwhile, were disporting in the dining-room, and when all the ladies, grand-mamma included, had sufficiently admired them, and they had returned to their nursery, Mrs. Owen bethought herself that she wished to speak confidentially to Miss Gay, or Laura, as she had determined in future to call her, on seeing Lord Flaxley's attentions so decided. To ' Laura,' she now added ' dear.'

"Laura, dear, I want to show you something," and the two ladies proceeded alone to the boudoir.

"I really wanted to have a little quiet chat with you," said Mrs. Owen, shutting the door after her, and seating Laura in a very easy chair.

"You say the Mowbrays are coming to the Dell, to-morrow. Now, do you think they would like to dine out the day following? I wish they would, for you know, Lord Flaxley is obliged to leave us for the Highlands, on Monday, and my mother and brother leave the same day. I wish you would all come on Saturday: it would make such a charming party. I suppose the Brocklebanks will leave you the day after the Mowbrays come, so I need not ask you to bring them."

"They are going to stay till Tuesday next, and if they are included in the invitation, I don't see how we could all manage to come;

yet, I am sure, we should none of us like to separate."

"No, of course not, but Laura dear, who are the Brocklebanks ?"

Laura slightly laughed as she replied,

"That is a question, I might with better reason ask you, if I had no touchstone of my own to determine who is who, for I met them, for the first time, at your house in town."

"Really, you surprise me, and did you form their acquaintance on so slight a foundation."

"I may again answer you with a sort of question. On what grounds did you form their acquaintance ?"

"Oh! simply because Mr. Owen thought their good-will of some consequence to us," replied Mrs. Owen, naïvely.

"I am now prepared with an answer for any one who will ask me, 'Who are the Brocklebanks ?'"

"And what is it?"

"This is it. Do you know Mr. and Mrs. Owen, of Llanbeddwr Hall, and of Eaton Square?—stylish people, I assure you. Well, the Brocklebanks are people of some consequence even to *them*, so judge what *I* consider them."

Mrs. Owen was perplexed. However, she had made up her mind to invite the Mowbrays to meet Lord Flaxley and her brother, with both of whom she knew they were acquainted, and greatly desiring to be introduced to Lady Cecilia's parties in town, she resolved that the Brocklebanks should not stand in the way; so, after a moment's appearance of reflection, she proposed to send her "omnibus" to fetch the large party from the Dell. The omnibus, bran-new as it was, with four good horses, could only do her credit with the Mowbrays; she therefore pressed Laura almost beyond refusal—at least, so Laura thought;

though, perhaps, the hope of again enduring the pleasing pain of meeting Charles Thornton, after so long a separation, might add something, in her idea, to the amount of pressure put upon her.

However that may have been, it was agreed between the two ladies, that Mrs. Owen should call the next day, after lunch, upon Lady Cecilia, to give her the invitation. Laura was sure her ladyship would not refuse it, because her talents and vivacity made society always agreeable to her, and if not absolutely the best, still, she enjoyed the best to be had, in whatever place she happened to be. This constant intercourse in varied circles, was a great cause of her success in society.

Having pleasantly arranged this little matter, the two ladies returned to the drawing-room, and found the gentlemen awaiting their appearance, to determine their immediate proceedings.

Mr. and Mrs. Gardiner, Miss Owen, and Mrs. Brocklebank were for exploring the poultry-yard, the orchard, and the kitchen-garden, and no fear of the heat deterred them from this improving tour.

Mrs. Owen devoted herself to the entertainment of Mr. Thornton, whom, she was surprised to find so heavy, and in this kind office she was joined by her youngest brother Roderick, an uninteresting boy, and Miss Brocklebank. However, she derived some satisfaction in the discovery that Mr. Thornton was intimate with the Mowbrays, and that Miss Brocklebank was a lady-like girl. Lord Flaxley and Miss Gay followed them towards the lake, and the latter was the only one of the party who seemed inclined to look at what they professed to have come to see. Dowager Lady Huntley and her daughter-in-law preferred remaining in the house. Mr. Brocklebank and Lord Huntley turned off into a bye path, to mount a little eminence from whence there was a good view of the Park; and Laura was left alone with Lord Flaxley, whose manner became now more indicative of admiration.

Laura longed to check it, for, far from gratifying, it only vexed her, and her disposition to be pleased was not increased by seeing Charles Thornton and Miss Brocklebank separate from the party in advance, to mount the rocky course of a stream, now nearly dry, and clad in ferns and verdure, which together with the exercise it afforded her of skipping from stone to stone, on the surest and prettiest of little feet, seemed to be its attraction to the young lady; while Mr. Thornton appeared quite satisfied to admire the vegetable beauties to which his companion called his attention, and to hold her pretty little hand, whenever she required help.

" By Jove," said Lord Flaxley, following the direction of Laura's eyes, " that's a pretty little friend of yours, Miss Gay, and her father is a millionaire, I suppose."

"Yes, I believe he is very wealthy— you must have seen him in the House."

"True, but I never remarked him—he never speaks, and you know there are as many cliques in the House, as in the town, only admission to them is a little more influenced by political and party interest. Had I known, what a fairy-like little girl he had for a daughter, perhaps I might have noticed him more.   Don't you think her very elegant ?"

"Yes," said Laura, with a sigh, and a sorry attempt at a smile.

"You can agree to such a remark, my dear Miss Gay, for to my mind, and, I believe, upon my conscience, all men of taste would support me, that *you* need never fear the judgment of Paris."

"I am not vain of my beauty," replied Laura, " I know what it is, and how long it may last, meanwhile, it shall serve me as well

as may be, but when it is gone, I trust I shall
be something, which, even now, happy and
fortunate though I seem, I might contemplate
with pride; it is to that something, I would
fain have my friends attach themselves."

The colour of her eyes deepened, and her
cheeks mantled with enthusiasm as she spoke,
for she was thinking of Charles Thornton,
though she addressed Lord Flaxley.

What is more infectious than enthusiasm?
This then, was the propitious signal—this the
stimulating moment when his lordship felt
himself equal to that effort of the intellect—
an acceptable offer; for an effort of the intellect, an offer must be; where passion in its
low and undiscriminating sense, and worldly
prudence are the motives, and affection
founded on heartfelt sympathy and harmony
of tastes is absent.

"Adorable girl! permit me to tell you,
how fervently I love you, how entirely our
sentiments accord on this, as on every other

subject—yes, indeed, your beauty *shall* serve you—it shall place you in a position you may contemplate with pride ; it shall not waste its sweetness on the desert air—it shall bloom— it shall grace a circle worthy of its charms."

Laura stopped, and drawing herself up to her full length, gazed at her admirer in silent amazement.

" Really, my lord, I was quite unprepared for this."

" No doubt, you were," continued his lordship, in blissful ignorance of her real sentiments. " Your peculiar modesty could hardly foresee a coronet; it is for me to tell you, how worthily you will wear it—it will be my happy lot to place it upon your brow."

Laura's face was suffused with blushes, but its expression was anything but promising.

" Have the goodness," said she, interrupting him, " to tell me what you are talking about. I hardly understand you. In plain language, are you asking me to marry you ?"

"Charming creature! dearest Laura! let me utter that sweetest of names; what am I telling you, but that I love you—you only— that I never have, and never shall love any other; and how disinterested my love, you yourself can judge. I am not noble after the fashion of Lord Huntley, without a *sous* to bless my poor nobility, but my fortune is equal to my birth."

"I hope, my lord, you are mistaken in the intensity and constancy of your love; indeed," she added with returning calmness, and a smile, " the fact that you have made no inquiry respecting my power of returning it, leads me to suspect that you have mistaken the nature of your own feelings. I trust and believe they are as transitory, as their declaration has been sudden. You must allow me, now, to thank you, for the honour you have conferred upon me, and to decline your offer in sober earnestness."

"Impossible! that a girl of your sense

Q 2

and judgment can refuse so advantageous an offer. Surely you can have no positive dislike to me—my morals— —my manners—my person—and even my opinions, you cannot think *them* exceptionable. Consider the position you would occupy; how much wider a sphere in which to shine—the rank you would enjoy. Surely, that father, whose memory you so much reverence, would have induced, you not overhastily to refuse me. Let me advise you in his name," pursued his lordship, with a tenderer and more modest accent.

"Thank you!" interposed Laura, with greater kindness, "for naming my dear father with respect, and now permit me, with all the frankness of friendship to state the difference of our views, on the important subject of love, and a position in life."

"To my mind, a marriage without love on both sides, is a base affront against nature; therefore wrong, and liable to suffering. It is not enough, that some passion should be felt on one side, and no aversion on the other; the esteem and affection should be mutual, and the deepest possible to each nature. Then, only, can the most perfect happiness be anticipated, because then only are the intentions of nature fulfilled. As regards the rank you offer, I do not covet it, nor can I see how it would benefit me. At present, I have access to as much of the society of intelligent and virtuous people as I have time to enjoy. Could I wish for more, in the way of society? Then as to the wider sphere for shining. It is, I apprehend, really, only a sphere in which to *shine*, and I have no desire to shine. I would rather work, where my reward may be the success of my labour, and not the praise of my efforts. If ever I marry, it will be to a man of similar sentiments, and my joy would be

to encourage his best efforts, and to cheer
him when the world frowned."

Lord Flaxley was silent; he was surprised, and his mind was revolving whether
with such sentiments, it would ever be
possible for Miss Gay to accept his father.

At this juncture, they came upon the
lake, and on its margin they saw Miss
Brocklebank and Charles Thornton coming
towards them, the latter laden with ferns.

"I have always thought," said his lordship, with a sigh of tender reverie, "that
Mr. Thornton was the man to suit you.
It is strange, that with so much in common,
you should so scrupulously avoid each other."

Laura's heart assented with a sigh, and
presenting her hand to Lord Flaxley, she said,

"I hope I may always have the honour
of considering you amongst my friends."

"Ever, dear Miss Gay," replied his lordship, pressing her hand gallantly to his lips.

Unfortunately for his peace, Thornton,

though still at some distance, saw the act.
Driven almost to frenzy, he was as docile
as a child in the hands of his pretty
companion; he did everything she wished
him, and assented to all her remarks.

When the two couples met, they were
forced into each other's company. Lord
Flaxley's admiration of the ferns Miss
Brocklebank had collected, and the compli-
ments he paid her, on the agility she had
displayed, in springing from rock to rock,
up the banks of the rivulet, were unbounded.

"Ah!" said Laura to herself, "that is
Lord Flaxley—superficial as the society of
which he is a member; once launched on
the stream of love, and borne on its current,
he will steer from object to object, until
acceptance arrests his course. Beauty is
his bark, and it always floats. But what
can Charles Thornton mean? Theresa
Brocklebank is not the girl he could really
love, pretty and amiable though she be.

She could not understand him; she could never work with him, and for him; and this is merely a dumb show on his part to break asunder every link remaining between us."

Thus musing, she lingered behind the others, until she was aroused by Miss Brocklebank's saying,

" Do you not admire ferns, Miss Gay ?"

" Yes," said Laura, rejoining them, with a determination not to be unjust towards her pretty little visitor, nor resentful towards Charles Thornton. "This maiden-hair," touching a specimen of that delicate plant, in the bundle which Charles Thornton was carrying, "is very pretty, and rare also."

" I wonder you don't make a fernery at the Dell; you have such a pretty little bit of cascade in your garden."

" *You* must make one," interrupted Lord Flaxley, addressing Miss Brocklebank, "and I will come to help you; I am sure Miss

Gay would be delighted to have such a memento of your taste."

They had now reached the house, and found the carriage waiting, and their friends assembled at the door.

"Let some one put up all those ferns for you," said Mrs. Owen.

"What beautiful specimens!" exclaimed Lord Huntley. "I did not know you had anything as beautiful as that in the country."

"You should really see the spot where I gathered them," replied Miss Brocklebank. "It is quite fairy-like. Indeed, Mr. Thornton says it is just from such a nook that Puck culls herbs to blind the fair Titania, and make her see love in the head of an ass."

Thornton's eyes met Laura's. Both of them coloured, and looked serious.

"So he has been quoting Shakespeare to her," thought Laura.

"She is as proud as Titania—blind," was Thornton's inward conclusion.

" Capital! what a wit you are, Thornton!"
exclaimed Lord Flaxley. " Upon my honour,
I do think some fairy bewitchment has happened to us all. Mrs. Owen, you are answer-
able for these midsummer-day dreams, wit-
ticisms, and *malencontres.*"

The whole party, with the addition of Lord
Flaxley, then set off for the Dell.

Miss Brocklebank informed Miss Owen of
the projected fernery; but on looking over
the bundle of ferns in the carriage, to her
disappointment, she found the one little root
of maiden-hair was missing.

" How provoking!" she exclaimed. " Mr.
Thornton is a most agreeable person; but he
certainly did not carry the ferns as carefully
as he might have done."

Had Laura Gay known of the missing fern,
what delight its absence would have given her !

Lord Flaxley talked incessantly to Mr.
Brocklebank; and though he admired Miss
Gay's horse and horsemanship, she had

abundant opportunities for silent reflections during the ride.

When Laura and her party had left the Hall, Lord Huntley proposed another stroll to Thornton, which the latter accepted with pleasure, in the hopes that Lord Huntley might be led to talk about Laura, and to give him some decisive information respecting her position with Lord Flaxley, and her sentiments towards himself.

Both gentlemen meditating the same subject, sauntered along in silence, broken only by common place remarks, in which neither took any interest.

At last, Lord Huntley said :

" What do you think of Flaxley ?   I think he was your *companion de voyage*, down here."

" Yes, he is good-natured and thoroughly *facile à vivre*, I should say,—can you tell me whether an engagement exists between him and Miss Gay ?"

" Indeed I cannot ; however, I hope not,

for they are totally unsuited to each other. I am very well acquainted with Miss Gay, and there are few women so capable of interesting me; yet, for Flaxley's sake, as well as her own, and I may say, for the sake of propriety, I should much regret to see her marry him. Beyond his facility, I have always understood, he has very little character. What he is, he is by birth, that is, traditionally; his opinions, his family pride, his morals, and his manners, are adventitious, and not a part of himself. Were he to marry a woman like Miss Gay, the force of her character would entirely upset his former self, and either he would become a mere puppet in her hands, to the vexation of his family, and his party, or he would act a part, full of inconsistency, in the attempt to reconcile his traditional belief, with her opinions and will. Indeed, whatever may be the discretion or power of a woman, and a wife, I never like to see it forced into a position, for which heaven did not intend it. I own it offends me to see the stronger vessel playing a subordinate part."

"Yet, I should fear, to the shame of our sex, that there are few men, who, as the husband of Miss Gay, would not find her will irresistible."

"Yes," replied his lordship, seriously, "that was once a painful consideration with me."

"Then you did once admire Miss Gay?" eagerly asked Thornton.

"Certainly, but my feelings were excited to admiration only, perhaps, because they received so little encouragement, for which, *now* I cannot be too grateful; few people could have been less suited to each other, than Miss Gay and myself. The wide scope of her opinions, and the fearlessness of her ventures into the regions of thought, would always have pained me; they might have attacked my prejudices, perhaps even my firmest convictions, and in a life of quietude, such as my profession necessitates, when the mind is made up, and the direction of all its motions fixed by habit, it is a dangerous thing even to lose one's prejudices, so intimately interwoven have they become with all one's moral consciousness."

" But Miss Gay is a religious person."

" No doubt; at heart, she is thoroughly religious. It is that which gives force and constancy to all her notions; but she is religious in her own way—a thorough independent; no forms bind her; she deems religion so natural a relation between God and man, that she suffers neither priest nor vail to intervene between her spirit and the Holy of Holies."

There was a pause. Perhaps *no man* likes to picture his mistress, the incarnation of a strong will, and an independent judgment.

" Your portrait of Miss Gay is not altogether a flattering one."

" No, and, indeed, it is quite one-sided; it was adapted to my own case, when I had to consider the objections to falling in love with her. The temptation to do so, none can doubt; her beauty, her grace, the depth of her feelings, her intelligence and truth, are enough to bewitch any man who should see much of her; and, I hardly doubt that Miss Gay is capable of so devoted an attachment to the object of her choice, as to become to *him* all he could wish—in fact, the very strength and constancy of her character are vouchers for that. Indeed, when evil is not the designed production of human perversity, a kind Providence always accords the antidote with the bane. But then, I cannot for a moment suppose that a man like Lord Flaxley could ever inspire her with any *real* attachment, and that is why I should so much regret to see them united; I heartily hope, and, indeed, believe, that no temptation of rank, or mere desire to settle in life, will induce her to accept one so unsuited to her."

Again there was a prolonged silence. Thornton, emboldened by Lord Huntley's candour and gentleness, felt that he was a man to be trusted, and longing to hear his account of what had passed at the Flower Show, he at length said:

"Perhaps, when we met at the Flower Show in Regent's Park, now, more than a year ago, it did not escape your lordship's observation, that Miss Gay was not an object of indifference to me?"

Lord Huntley looked earnestly in his face, and replied:

"Do you wish me to answer you with perfect openness?"

"I do."

"Well then, I concluded, from your manner, that you had once been attached to Miss Gay; but that some more recent passion had overcome that attachment, and rendered even its remembrance disagreeable."

"Good Heavens! surely, *she* did not view my conduct in that light. What a fool—what a wretch I have been, in a momentary fit of jealousy to cast away the happiness of my life. Indeed, she was mistaken—utterly mistaken. Never was she more dear to me, than at that moment."

Lord Huntley had been convinced, that Laura *was* attached, and devotedly attached, to Charles Thornton. How far she had been able to overcome this affection, he knew not; and he never would have confided his persuasion of its former existence to any one, had not his sympathy for Thornton been strongly excited by his outburst of grief, and his agonized tones, which took him quite by surprise.

"Your mode of showing your affection was, I am sure, exquisitely painful to its object, and, as a mere observer, it conveyed to *me* the idea of aversion."

"But why had she left the tent, where first I saw her, and where I sought to meet her again?"

"Because your want of alacrity disappointed her, and she was, moreover, not a little shocked to hear, from Lady Cecilia Mowbray, an unfavourable rumour respecting your intimacy with Mrs. Redford, which, you must admit, was that day rather confirmed than refuted by appearances."

Thornton groaned, and, after a pause, replied:

"If such a rumour did prevail, there was not a particle of foundation for it. Whatever her husband may have been, Mrs. Redford is not, and never was, a friend of mine."

Had Thornton been now assured of Laura's engagement to Lord Flaxley, he would have written her an explanation of his past conduct, and a final adieu, and he would immediately have quitted Llanbeddwr. But, notwithstanding appearances, he would

not believe in such an engagement, and he
strengthened himself in his unbelief by Lord
Huntley's opinion, and by the emotion at
meeting him, slight as it was, which Laura
had manifested in the boudoir: he, therefore,
determined to remain at Llanbeddwr a few
days longer, in order to satisfy himself on
the subject most essential to his happiness.

During dinner that day, Lord Flaxley
was incessant in his praises of the Dell
It was a fairy spot, all fragrance and flowers,
precisely such an one as lovers would choose
to woo in. The Brocklebanks, too, were
excellent people—so intelligent; in fact, it
seemed to every one at table, and to Thornton
among the rest, that Lord Flaxley's admiration of Miss Gay was expansive beyond all
the proprieties of love.

Mrs. Owen wondered how the Mowbrays
would like to meet the Brocklebanks, and
whispered to Mr. Thornton her own impression of Miss Gay's oddities. He assured

her that the Mowbrays enjoyed the society of sensible people, quite irrespective of conventional classification.

"Indeed," he added, "both Mr. Mowbray and his wife are themselves so thoroughly agreeable and sensible, and so well connected, that every set receives them gladly on their own terms. They are, therefore, unshackled, and free to please themselves."

"And you might occupy such a position as their's, Thornton," remarked Lord Flaxley, "if you would cast aside your solemnity, and resume the facility and *bonhommie*, which, I hear, once enhanced your intellectual *agrémens*."

"Age," replied Thornton, attempting a laugh, "makes great ravages on one's gaiety."

"Oh, yes; I dare say, one year counts two in some men's gravity. For my part, I am a laughing philosopher, like Miss Gay."

Dinner was late, and the evening short, Thornton was even graver than usual, and every one was, or professed to be, uncommonly sleepy with the exercise, and the excessive heat of the day. Bed was welcome to all. To Thornton, it brought hours of undisturbed meditations. To Mr. and Mrs. Owen, a conversation on their social affairs, terminating, like most of such conversations, in no result. To Lord Flaxley, cheerful dreams, wherein Laura Gay and Miss Brocklebank figured by turns.

" How happy could I be with either,
Were t'other dear charmer away."

CHAPTER VI.

THE following day was uneventful. The Mowbrays arrived for lunch at the Dell. Mrs. Owen and most of her party called upon them; but as the gentlemen were mounted, and had planned rather a long ride, their call, *en passant*, was very short.

Lady Cecilia was both entertained and pleased with Mr. Brocklebank, and Susan was just as much charmed with Miss Brocklebank.

All the Brocklebanks were in raptures with the Mowbrays, especially with Lady Cecilia.

Having said thus much, we leave to the

fertile fancy of the reader the *entretiens*, agreeable and edifying, which doubtless distinguished the first day's intimacy of these worthy and amiable persons; proceeding ourselves to the Saturday morning, the day fixed for the dinner at the Hall. Of course, it was fine—our memory treasures up none but sunny days, save and except those whereon an ill wind blew us some good. Susan Mowbray and Theresa Brocklebank were walking altogether in the shade, after breakfast, comparing notes respecting their various singing, dancing, drawing and other masters, and telling such anecdotes as amuse fair young ladyhood, when Mr. Brocklebank came up and joined them.

" Well, young ladies, if modern masters can produce anything so enchanting as Lady Cecilia Mowbray, I shall join you in celebrating their praises; but I suspect nature has more to do with such lovely productions than art.

" Non so ben dire s'adorna o se negletta,
    Se caso od arte il volto compose
    Di natur d'amor del cielo amici,
    Le sue negligenze sono gli artifici."

exclaimed Miss Brocklebank.

Susan was delighted—she had read the lines in Tasso herself, and now wondered that she had never applied them to her mamma.

" Bravo," exclaimed Mr. Brocklebank, for though he knew nothing of Tasso, beyond his existence as a poet, he understood Italian, having resided a year in Trieste, before his marriage.

This apt quotation was exactly reported by Susan to her papa, from whom it went direct to Lady Cecilia, and proved an irresistible passport of good-will between Theresa Brocklebank and herself. It was also repeated by Miss Brocklebank herself to Laura and Lord Flaxley in the evening.

The former admired its opposite description, and the latter, the young maiden herself, for having merited the approbation of so good a judge as Laura Gay.

The omnibus came to the Dell for Miss Gay and her party. The drive was a merry one; for Lady Cecilia, Mr. Mowbray, and Mr. Brocklebank, kept up the ball of conversation with spirit, and their audience was intelligent.

Laura alone remained silent and abstracted. She was revolving the chances of an opportunity of telling Charles Thornton in a calm and friendly way, that if he wished the tacit promises exchanged between them at Rome and at Veii, to be cancelled, she was ready to do her part towards freeing him. She rather hoped Mrs. Owen would send her in to dinner with him. Then, she thought, " amidst the din of conversation, I will muster courage sufficiently to say a few words which he cannot misunderstand."

Before dinner, Lord Huntley talked to her

with the freedom of an old friend. He spoke
with kindness and approbation of Thornton,
expressing his sorrow at seeing him so
depressed ; this touched Laura herself so
much, that when dinner was announced,
she trembled lest Thornton should be appointed to escort her, and earnestly prayed
in her heart, that Mrs. Owen would send
her in with Lord Huntley. That lady, however, told Lord Flaxley to take her, and she
found herself seated at table betwixt him and
Lord Huntley. On the other side of Lord
Flaxley, sat Miss Brocklebank and Mr.
Thornton.

The latter was evidently out of spirits and
absent, and he barely replied to his fair
partner's numerous questions and remarks.
Fortunately for her enjoyment, she had
Lord Flaxley on the other side, who finding
Miss Gay, though perfectly civil and friendly,
rather taciturn, devoted himself, at last, entirely to the entertainment of the fair The-

resa. Lord Huntley divided his attentions equally between Mrs. Brocklebank and Miss Gay; and, perhaps, their conversation was the quietest and least reproachable of any at the table, for mirth or originality.

Mrs. Owen was in full feather, and made herself as charming as she could to Mr. Mowbray, who pronounced her, in his own mind, quite unfitted for her station in life. Accustomed to the society of a woman like Lady Cecilia, Mrs. Owen's conversation and affectation bored him excessively, and he caught himself almost uttering aloud Burns's lines,

> O wad some pow'r the giftie gie us,
> To see oursels as others see us!
> It wad frae monie a blunder free us,
> In dress and gait, and e'en devotion."

Still more in society, where we may safely say, no two things can differ more entirely than our estimate of self, and the estimation in which we are held. Such were

Mr. Mowbray's reflections, while, in the simplicity of her vanity, Mrs. Owen imagined he must be drawing a comparison highly favourable to herself, between her own polished manners, and the simplicity of Miss Gay's, or the homeliness of Mr. Brocklebank's. Alas! for the reward of those who seek honour of men—what a speculation it is!

After dinner, Mrs. Owen was not so happy; for Lady Cecilia had heard a tolerably correct account of her from Laura, Mrs. Brocklehank, and Miss Owen. She did not, therefore, honour her with overmuch attention; and poor Mrs. Owen made several ineffectual attempts to edge a refined remark into the conversation, which Mrs. Brocklebank, Lady Cecilia, young Lady Huntley, and Miss Owen were conducting on the simple principles of common sense and spontaneous wit.

Lord Flaxley and Lord Huntley were

the first to join the ladies; and they were immediately followed by all the other gentlemen, Mr. Mowbray, Mr. Thornton, and Mr. Owen excepted.

"I cannot make out young Thornton," observed Mr. Brocklebank to his wife, as he seated himself behind her and Lady Cecilia Mowbray, "his gravity is quite unnatural at his age, and it seems accompanied by melancholy and suffering; I should fear, either that some pecuniary misfortune threatened him, or that he was oppressed by wounded affections, or by some serious bodily ailment."

Lady Cecilia's eyes wandered towards Laura, who, on overhearing the remark, had turned pale; flushing again to the very tips of her fingers, as Thornton entered the room.

Presently her ladyship moved close to the table, where Laura was mechanically turning the leaves of a book of engravings, and said in a voice audible only to Laura

herself, "you really should forgive him, dear
—this mutual torture is quite wrong."

"Oh! I do," whispered Laura, "with all
my heart! I wish you would tell him so."

Lady Cecilia smiled, and shook her head,
"*That* you must do yourself."

Miss Brocklebank played and sang
charmingly, and Lord Flaxley listened with
much more attention than he had manifested when the Miss Simkins's, and their
brother attempted to entertain him in a
similar way.

Laura thought the evening eternal, and
yet she regretted every moment that passed,
for it left her with a chance the less of
saying what she had determined to say to
Charles Thornton. Every time that he seemed
to be on the point of approaching her,
some other person was sure to come up
to speak to her. Nothing could be more
trying, and when the party broke up, her
face wore an expression of vexation and

regret, which rendered it quite unlike itself.

It so happened, that Charles Thornton stood close to the door, as she and her party passed out of the drawing-room. Laura hurriedly extended her hand to him, and as he stooped to take it, she said, with a calmness that surprised her.

"I am sorry I have had no opportunity of speaking to you this evening."

Charles Thornton scarcely touched her fingers, and his look expressed nothing but bewilderment. What could she mean! Could it be that his excellent, and really noble friend, Lord Huntley, whom, for a brief period, he had almost hated, as a rival, had been acting the mediator. When he warmly grasped Lord Huntley's hand, to wish him good night, and felt that grasp as warmly returned, he was convinced of the truth of his surmise, and vowed a gratitude, deeper far, than Redford's supposed loan had ever inspired.

In the silence of his own chamber, that night, Charles Thornton relieved from the too oppressive burthen of his sorrow, and restored, as he fondly dared to think, to hope, and life, and love, did not forget to offer up, at the shrine of his Maker, the tribute of his heart.

CHAPTER VII.

SUNDAY, the day of rest, had come, when in our happy land, the children of luxury and leisure are recalled from the aimless round of gaiety and amusement, to calmer and more serious feelings; while the men and women of business and of toil, derive from tranquil rest, and religious hopes, a sounder state of mind and a recreated body. No doubt, there are, also, the sons and daughters of perdition, whose body is their god, and for them, Sunday is but one of that sum of days, which leads down to the lowest depths of moral degradation.

But, few of this wretched class, of our

brethren dwelt in the secluded vale of Llanbeddwr, indeed, as we have said before, the population was small, and the shepherd active and beloved.

Laura Gay rose early this Sunday morning. It was the anniversary of her birthday. This day, twelve months ago, she had sat despairingly under the lime tree, almost desiring death to remove her from a desert world. How changed her feelings now! life had become more than tolerable—cheerful, useful. The very sense of being which activity calls forth, was a pleasure to her; and she accepted, gratefully, life with its clouds and its sunshine.

The acuteness of her grief, too, at the loss of Thornton's affection, how much that had worn off! Still she felt she must ever love him, and consider that his desertion had rendered her happiness in life less complete, than it otherwise might have been.

"To-day," said she, "shall be a fresh

era in my life. To-day, I will strengthen and establish myself in relinquishing every remaining portion of passion, and either by word or letter, I will shortly release him from the scruples of conscience, which, while they prove him to be a man of honour, are grievous obligations."

Laura occupied the room in which her aunt had died; and she was now seated in the small dressing-room where she had almost lived during Mrs. Owen's illness. This Sunday, a year and a day ago, she had been summoned to partake, with her aunt, of that memorial repast which symbolizes the intimate union of souls departed with souls on earth, and their still more intimate relation to the eternal Captain of our Salvation. Deeply musing on these matters, she seemed clearly to see the transient nature of earthly passions, even of that human love, which, though it borrow the glories of our immortal souls, and combine so harmoniously with all our noblest and holiest virtues, is still a passion we share in common with the animal creation.

What then, is this passion common or unclean? God forbid! Every law He has clothed in mortal flesh, call we it, passion, reason, intellect, or imagination, is pure and holy, so it develop itself within its appointed limits, and infringe not other laws of equal right. What shall we say then? Are we bound to exercise each faculty of our nature to its complete development? Not so; we have long lost the power of entire individual perfection. Race, custom, education, the long struggles of human life, the faults and vices of our neighbours, have all combined to circumscribe and deform us. Paradise we have lost, and virtue walketh among stony places. Still some little remains in our power; and Heaven with all freedom lies before us.

If we may not love, we may feel friendship, and friendship, sure, is akin to heavenly charity, and endureth for ever. Still, though Laura Gay's love had stopped short in its course, and disappointment had taken its place, though she blamed herself for having given up her whole soul to the all-absorbing passion, she could not, and did not regret that she had experienced it. How strong within us, and how constant is our desire for the knowledge of good and evil. These meditations and moralizings, gave a sedate and Sunday air to her manner and countenance when she descended to breakfast, and so sincere was it, that it communicated itself to all her friends.

The morning was balmy and inviting, and the two gentlemen and their daughters agreed to walk to church. The elder ladies drove there, and it was arranged by Laura and Miss Owen, that the whole party, with the exception of herself, should return in the carriage. It was Sacrament Sunday, and Laura particularly wished to stay, for she felt, that on this occasion, the divine repast would, indeed, be to her a commemoration and a consolation; therefore, she said, she would return on foot, and that they were not to wait lunch for her.

The small church of Llanbeddwr was a plain building outside, and still more primitive within. It was, in fact, originally a chapel of ease to the church of Glynsbrynn. It contained but two pews, one belonging to the Owens of Llanbeddwr, and the other to the incumbent. The remainder of the congregation sat on chairs and benches.

" The morning service was conducted in English, and usually attended by the families from the Hall and the Dell, with their servants and English dependents, by some of their chief tenants, by the most intelligent portion of the surrounding peasantry, and by the school-children, whom Mr. Gardiner took care to instruct chiefly in English.

The afternoon service was always in Welsh,

and solely attended by those parishioners who could only understand their native tongue. No family monuments or tombs occupied the space to which the living hearers of the Word are best entitled, or forced upon their minds those trivial distinctions that nourish arrogance, pride, and servility, and breed envy, hatred, and malice in the world, but which have no existence beyond the tomb.

All was cleanliness, simplicity, and light, thanks to Miss Gay's provisions, and Mrs. Gardiner's vigilance. No Gothic shades or mystic hues encouraged the mind of the disciple to wander from the familiar teaching of the Lord, or turned *that* which those who run may read, into mysteries above and beyond the nature of man. Lord Huntley preached; and his short discourse acccorded well with the simplicity around. The topics he treated were those which characterize Christianity—single-mindedness, truth, purity, charity, and the forgiveness of sins.

"Come then," said the preacher, "let us eat of the Eucharist, knowing that we are fellow-heirs of immortality, nourished with the same food, and partakers of the same promises. No longer slaves to the unknown powers of darkness, we are freed from the fears of superstition, the worship of fate, or the deification of matter. For we have a God and Father, whose power is such, that to Him these things are as though they were not."

"Let us claim His fellowship, and accept the simple tokens of His love. For, as He nourishes our bodies with earthly food, so he feeds our spirits on the bread of life. Is it wonderful, then, that the law-giver of mind should also dispose of matter? What miracle do we ask to prove it? Look abroad! for the proof is before our eyes. To *whom* is it given to triumph over nature, to bind and loose its mighty powers, to unlock its secret laws; but to those whose civilization is

Christian, and whose regenerated hearts make combination and good-will among men, forbearance, patience, and justice possible.

"To those, whose ken does not extend, beyond their native vale, or their own generation, we would propose a still easier and better test. Let them regulate their lives according to the precepts of Christ, and fill their hearts with His love; and they will soon become assured by experience that heaven and earth are theirs, if they are His.

"They may then sit down to that table of celebration, to enjoy its spiritual cheer, with hearts full of joy, friendship and gratitude."

The sermon had some effect upon all present, although truth bids us say, that throughout its course Mrs. Owen's eyes frequently wandered to the bonnets and mantles of the party from the Dell: Mr. Owen gazed on the broad shoulders of Mr.

Brocklebank, with an intensity that had reference chiefly to his own slate quarries; and Lord Flaxley satisfied himself by attentive observation, that, if Miss Gay's head and throat were set upon Miss Brocklebank's ample bust, the palm of beauty, according to his taste, would belong to the latter.

Thornton listened with profound attention, and when the sermon was over, he remained like Laura for the Sacrament, and they knelt together, at the table of the Lord: that time-honoured table which can derive no sanctity from wood or stone of cunning workmanship, or from coverings of fine linen and purple curiously wrought—no, nor yet from consecration by priestly hands; all it has of holiness, must be brought thither in the loving hearts and faithful memories of those who meet there to celebrate a common brotherhood with the Divine High Priest, and to claim a fulfilment of His promise of that immortality, towards which human hope and desire constantly point. The table of the Lord may be found, glorious indeed, where neither priest, nor ecclesiastical edifice ever existed, so divine and so spiritual is its import.

Laura was one of the first to issue from the church, and wishing to be alone in her homeward walk, she chose rather a circuitous path to the Dell, one that led high on the breast of the mountain, and was, in fact, no regular communication at all, but merely a sheep walk, leading to the summit of the moor, with various descents, branching off in its upward progress, one of which at a considerable height, led down, in zig-zag fashion, to the farm-yard at the back of the Dell.

Thornton had followed Laura out of church, but he had been obliged to stay a few minutes to speak to Mrs. Gardiner, who kindly invited him to lunch at the parsonage, along with Lord Huntley, who was staying to hear the Welsh sermon in the afternoon. This he declined, and standing thoughtfully a moment beneath a sycamore that overshadowed the churchyard stile, through which Laura had just passed, he was thus accosted by old John.

"Please, Sir, this is not the way to the Hall, may be you'd like a lad to go along with you."

"No, no thank you," replied Thornton, gazing after Laura.

A faint smile played on old John's features, as, with hat in hand, and long lank white hair blowing about his face, he pointed to the path she was ascending, and said; "well, Sir, if you only want a fine mountain walk, and a pretty sight, you can't do better nor follow that there young lady, who knows best of all where there's sommut worth looking at."

"Thank you," replied Thornton, striding up the path, at a pace calculated only to accelerate the beatings of his heart.

"Eh! look there now Maria, did I ever! that's just the way with all o 'em young ones; they knows nought about taking it quietly, I don't mane to say as our missus is'nt worth it all, and he's as nice a young gentleman as I ever see'd; he's a sort of a sensible look, like, sommut of our master; mind my words, she'll have none o' that fine young lord; the like o' him's not fit for she."

Maria and her father were not, by any means, admirers of the aristocracy. The people of the Hall represented that class to them, and they disapproved of the way in which Mr. and Mrs. Owen managed both their property and their household. They had not, consequently, at all approved of the exaltation the younger servants at the Dell manifested, when they opined that Miss Gay would shortly become Lady Flaxley; and Thornton, although entirely a stranger to old John, had his best wishes for the success of his suit.

When he had almost come up with Laura, he slackened his pace to regain courage for an interview, which might prove either the happiest, or the bitterest moment of his life, and must prove one of extraordinary excitement.

Laura knew not that she was followed, and walking slowly along, absorbed in serene and consoling meditations, she at last stopped to rest herself for a moment on a favourite mossy bank, a little raised above the swardy path, and embosomed in ferns and furze.

Here she had often enjoyed solitude, or, better still, the sole sweet company of brother or father. Hither human beings seldom came, and neither parish path, nor public road beguiled the thoughts into the regions of the every day world. Nothing of the neighbourhood, save the point of the church belfry, and the tops of some trees above the Dell, was visible from this spot, which had seemed to Laura's childish fancy like a halt betwixt Heaven and earth.

As she seated herself, her eye fell upon Thornton, now only a few yards behind her. There he was. At length, the decisive moment, of late, so ardently desired, had come; a quieter spot, or a more convenient opportunity for explanation and friendly reconciliation could hardly have been discovered. Laura had but a few moments for preparation, and after imbibing copious draughts of pure mountain air, taking the initiative, she rose to meet him.

"I know why you seek me," said she, with kind composure, "your feelings of honour prompt you to ask a release from the over-hasty attachment to which you gave utterance in Rome. I give it you now, freely, and with it, I forgive you all the pain which your words at the Flower

Show, and your subsequent estrangement have caused me."

She dared not look up in his face, to note the effect her words produced; indeed, her own eyes were blinded with tears, and she was conscious, that towards the last her voice had faltered. However, drawing in courage with another long breath, and offering him her hand, she continued:

"Now, we are friends. I can no longer stand between you and happiness."

The hand she offered was strangely dealt with, considering the sense of her words. That it was no longer her own, she was forced to believe, by its wandering to her lover's lips and heart.

"*You* stand betwixt me and happiness!" he exclaimed. "*You* are my happiness! Release me! *Forgive* me—oh! never release me, if you prize my happiness, and let me keep this hand in token of your forgiveness."

Her hand so frankly offered, and so quickly lost, remained in the embrace of its new owner, but the hearts of both were too full for utterance, and they sat down on the bank in a transport of renewed love. Tears of joy streamed down Laura's cheeks, Charles Thornton, too, was overcome with emotion. But as nature teaches us to cast a veil over the fondest effusions of loving hearts, we will not transcribe the terms of endearment whicb broke from the lips of either, ere they could regain sufficient calmness to explain to each other the causes of their long estrangement, and the doubts, fears, and accidents which had interposed to prolong it. Suffice it to say, that nothing could exceed Laura's surprise on hearing that he had written to her so soon after the Flower Show. How greatly such a letter would have alleviated the bitter agony she endured during her aunt's last illness ! Charles's surprise equalled her own, when he heard that not *that* letter, but the letter addressed to his unknown friend of the loan, was the only one which had ever reached her.   Great was his indignation against Mrs. Redford, for he doubted not but that she had intercepted his letter; and when Laura told him how, at Folkestone, she had been tortured by her insinuations respecting the loan, his displeasure was at its height; but amidst so much joy, how could displeasure last?—Mrs. Redford and her sins were soon forgotten in the presence of his beloved mistress, and of happiness and love so complete, and so suddenly restored.

Time flew unheeded, and, perhaps, the discourse of the lovers might have been prolonged, until the western sun had bathed the mountain side, and themselves, in golden light, had not old John's blue plush and livery buttons appeared in the direction of the Dell. Miss Owen had become uneasy, especially after learning from old John that Laura

had set off home immediately on quitting
church, and he was despatched, a willing
messenger, to seek the stray lamb. His
young mistress was dear to him, as any
of his own brood, and when he met her
hanging on Charles Thornton's arm, and observed the expression of both their countenances, he guessed what had passed between
them. Strong emotion was evident in the
old man's face as he thus addressed the young
couple.

"Miss Owen was uneasy, Miss. God bless
you! my dear young lady! I hope Sir, as
you'll always be good to her. I hope as
you'll turn out like our master as was, Sir,
for she's always lived among good folk and
kind, Sir."

" Upon my soul, I will devote my life to
her happiness, and to the service of God, my
excellent friend," replied Thornton, grasping
old John's hand with a warmth indicative of
his earnestness. The faithful servant turned

homeward to announce his mistress at the Dell, and every now and then the back of his hand was passed over his eyes to brush away the tiny tear of old age.

As they drew near the house, Laura's mind reverted to Miss Owen, and she said to Charles:

"Miss Owen has been a good friend to me in my troubles: now, that I am happy, I must be faithful to her; I cannot bear to think of suffering her to resume her solitary life. Let us both treat her with affection and respect."

"Oh yes! she shall always live with us," replied Thornton fervently. "I could love and respect twenty such old maids, dearest, for your sake."

So intoxicated were they both with the bliss of joy, following on so long a period of apparently hopeless separation, that they were quite unequal to facing the world, even in the pleasant form of a room full of friends.

Thornton, however, gallantly took upon himself to appear in public, whilst Laura escaped to her room.

We will not attempt to relate the interesting figure he cut, the absurd answers he gave respecting his walk, his want of politeness, or his awkwardness in saluting the party.

The Mowbrays smiled at each other, and the Brocklebanks stared. Laura sent for Miss Owen, who presently reappearing with red eyes, asked Thornton to take some refreshment in the dining-room, where she received, in Laura's presence, so chivalrous a declaration of his esteem and devotion as went far to thaw the ice of her live-long virginhood. When she rejoined the party in the drawing-room, she found Lady Cecilia informing the astonished Brocklebanks of the state of affairs.

The pretext of lunch lasted until Williams made his appearance to lay the cloth for dinner: then Laura was obliged to retreat to dress;

and in her own room she received the cordial
congratulations of Lady Cecilia, a sisterly
salute from Theresa and Susan, and a motherly
one from Mrs. Brocklebank.

Dinner was on the point of being announced, when Lord Flaxley made his appearance, as he said, in search of Thornton,
who had been found missing since noon, and
whose non-appearance had caused some uneasiness to the host and hostess at Llanbeddwr. His lordship had come on horse-
back, followed by a groom leading a horse,
for the truant guest. He was invited to stay
dinner, and he was much inclined to accept
the invitation; however, consideration for the
party at Llanbeddwr prevailed, and he pro-
tested he must return immediately accompanied by Thornton.

The leave-taking between the lovers, and
the looks of the bystanders, informed him
how matters stood. He was not so much
mortified as he might have been, had Miss

Brocklebank not been present: besides, his
sagacity was flattered, when he remembered
how he had told Thornton and Miss Gay,
that they were just suited to each other, and
he determined to accompany Thornton to
the Dell the following morning for the
pleasure of telling Miss Brocklebank how
strong his presentiments on the subject had
been. The two young men mounted, and
sent the groom on before at a gallop to announce their return to the Hall.

"Well," said Lord Flaxley, after trotting
for several minutes, in a silence he hoped
Thornton would break. "I wish you joy,
my dear fellow, of a conquest worthy of you;
but surely it is not the result of these few
day's acquaintance."

"No" replied his companion, "it is only
the renewal of an old engagement."

"Is it possible? How could you both
avoid each other, and behave as you did.
Upon my soul, you philosophers are a very

extraordinary race, and if I were not the best fellow in the world, I declare, upon my honour, I should think you had both used me very ill in not acquainting me with your engagement."

"But *you are* the best fellow in the world, my lord," rejoined Thornton

"Come, come, don't my lord me, Thornton. There's no reason why we should not be friends; after all, I have only paid your lady-love the highest compliment a man can pay a woman, and I found her cold as ice. It is true, she might have made her refusal a little more flattering, by telling me the real reason of it: however, she is an excellent creature, and I am not the man to blame a beauty, be she never so cruel."

"I am sure Miss Gay was sensible of the honour you did her, and I have no doubt she has a great regard for you."

"Nonsense, Thornton, she was not at all sensible of the honour, I do assure you;

however, I do believe she regards me as a friend."

" I have no doubt she does, and you deserve to be treated as one."

" Bravo ! let us clap hands on that. The bargain struck, we are fast friends."

They shook hands, and Lord Flaxley's merry laugh roused the sylvan echoes of the woods, as they rode through the Park of Llanbeddwr.

" Let *me* tell the news," said he, as they dismounted at the Hall door; and it was agreed he should do so.

Lord Huntley did not seem at all surprised. Mrs. Owen could hardly recover from her astonishment, and it increased still more when she found that Lord Flaxley was ready to put off his Highland journey on the pretext of looking after Thornton, if invited to prolong his stay at the Hall. Lord Flaxley was too hearty a lover of fuss, fun and importance, not to enjoy the present conjuncture. Besides, the wave of love which had failed to bear him into the arms of Laura Gay, was on the point of depositing him at the feet of Theresa Brocklebank. In fact, he had made up his mind (without a moment's doubt of his free agency and powers of persuasion) so to dispose Thornton and Miss Gay, as to make them ask him to act as groomsman, and Theresa Brocklebank as bridesmaid; not that he had as yet determined to lead that young lady to the altar as his bride — no — he would make enquiries respecting her fortune—he would sound the old gentleman's intentions—he would study more closely her manners and character. These prudent resolutions, carried out by a man of Lord Flaxley's temperament, could hardly help ending in love.

However, having brought one love story to a satisfactory conclusion, it is not our intention to carry our reader through a second, for the pleasing purpose of proving that the course of true love may run smooth, even though difference of rank should be a seeming obstacle.

Let us here dismiss Lord Flaxley's good-natured and accommodating passion, by saying that his stay at Llanbeddwr was regulated by that of the Brocklebank's at the Dell: and that he gained his point in being chosen second groomsman with Theresa Brocklebank as second bridesmaid at Laura's marriage —that settlements were negotiated between himself and Mr. Brocklebank, and that all the Brocklebanks, father and sons, came forward most handsomely to bestow a magnificent portion on the child, whose marriage would connect them with the aristocracy. Mrs. Brocklebank, alone, withheld for a time her complete approbation of the match, not because it somewhat diminished her son's prospects, but because, she said, it was so inconsistent.

Lord Helston was furious, when first he heard that his son had a second time fixed his choice without consulting him. But what, in such a case could a noble tenant for life do? And his lordship's ire was gradually appeased, by the beauty, grace and fortune of his daughter-in-law; whilst Lady Mary was never tired of repeating the remark:

" Well, after all, it is not so bad as marrying an actress."

In due time Lady Flaxley occupied as distinguished a place in the beau-monde as any of the former Ladies Flaxley and Countesses Helston had ever done; while her good temper, good sense and good looks, and her husband's constant affection and respect for her, made her the darling of the family. We have thus briefly disposed of these interesting young people, that we may return to our lovers, unembarrassed with any but their concerns.

Monday morning—of all Monday mornings the most consciously happy to Charles Thornton and Laura Gay—rose cheerily bright. The breakfast table had scarcely

been cleared, ere Charles appeared at the
Dell, and considerate friends soon permitted
the lovers to be alone.

" I have a confused recollection, dearest
Laura, that you said yesterday, you had received a letter of mine respecting the loan—
can it be that *you* were my friend in need."

" I was a minor then, but at my suggestion, my dear aunt willingly lent you the
money. She died happy in the conviction of our
constant affection, and believing that she had
done what she could to promote our union.
You shared with me her latest prayers and
blessings." Laura was too deeply affected
to proceed, and leaning against her lover's
shoulder, to hide her emotion, she heard the
deep drawn sighs in which he poured out
gratitude and fond regrets to the memory of
her departed aunt. After a short pause,
she continued : " When I became her re-
presentative, I received your letter of thanks."

" The suggestion was yours," at length
he broke forth ; " kindest, and dearest, and

best of friends, how was it I did not think of you? Why did you not claim my gratitude?"

"Because I did not want that. I wished to promote your happiness and independence— and I loved you. Those are still my feelings —let us be grateful to Heaven for the good things we enjoy, and for each other's love."

"I begin to understand the error of my own feelings, dearest Laura, I adored you more than I loved you, though that, too, was in no small degree, but I made an idol of you, in my imagination, conjuring up the poetic images of passion, and losing sight of the true, hearty, really serviceable woman that you are. Fancy plays us false as well as reason : besides, the idola of the mind which mislead our judgment, there are idola of the heart framed by passion and fancy. Let us eschew both, and in the midst of our bliss, take truth only to dwell with us."

A brief period of mutual confidences confirming their mutual love and plighted faith was allowed to pass, and then it became necessary to fix the day of their union; for the world without ever presses us to fulfil our destiny and its own.

The Brocklebanks and the Mowbrays could not prolong their visit at the Dell, but promising to re-assemble there for a certain event, they begged that an approximate day might be named.

Old John insisted it should be soon, for the sake of having the finest fruit and flowers to furnish forth the wedding feast.

Mrs. Slater thought the trousseau would take some time to prepare; whereas Laura saw no necessity for a trousseau at all. Miss Owen, though very busy, gave it as her candid opinion, that there would be an impropriety in marrying without a trousseau, but she thought its completion before the wedding an immaterial point on the present occasion. The majority, among whom we may reckon the lovers themselves, were unfavourable to delay; however, as Thornton

insisted upon settling the whole of Laura's
property upon herself, Mr. Jenkins's expe-
dition in preparing the settlements determined the day.

Ere long, the Dell and the Hall were again
the scene of bustle and society, and even the
parsonage furnished a room or two for the
marriage guests. The wedding was pronounced a very pretty one; and it was a
very happy one, for no one feared the results.
Of course, tears were shed during the ceremony. Old John wept, because his master
" as was," was not there to see it. Miss
Owen because it was to take away her dear
Laura, her adopted child for a month;
Lady Cecilia because she was easily excited,
and Theresa Brocklebank, she hardly knew
why, but perhaps from sympathy.

The happy couple set off on a tour—they
did not care whither, but as both were utilitarians, as well as happy lovers and people of
taste, a few days of the honeymoon were
spent in town, in the choice of a residence.

CHAPTER VIII.

Two years have now elapsed.

Charles and Laura have just come down from town, and they are seated under the stately lime, reading and talking together. Miss Owen begins to think herself too old to work for Missionary baskets, so she knits socks, and does crotchet trimmings for baby's frocks. The evangelical magazine she still takes in, but her greatest of religious exertion, is the evangelizing of baby Thornton's nurse. She studies infant sanitation, treatises on education, and baby literature, and she has almost completed the first volume of " Calico Scrap Books."

Mr. and Mrs. Thornton have just come down to the Dell, and, as we have said, they are seated beneath the stately lime. Their cup of happiness is full, they have nothing to wish for, but much to do. Charles's spirits are buoyant still, and Laura is gay, yet both their countenances have assumed a new expression of serious gentleness, that makes their friends observe how like each other they are growing.

They are talking over the time they have spent since their marriage—balancing the good and evil they have done—drawing wisdom from failures, and courage from success. Sweet, indeed, is such communion and counsel between intelligent beings, where love and candour preside.

> " Par mo venieno i tuoi pensier tra i miei,
>   Con simile atto e con simile faccia,
>   Sì che d'entrambi un sol consiglio fei."

And if those sceptics, whose eyes have so long gazed on matter, that they can no longer see ought else in man, could once enter with heart and soul into such bliss as this, they would come to say, that the soul of man, and the polypus are not of common origin, or of the same texture; and that such high counsel and holy joy are something more than the fortuitous concourse of atoms without durability and inspiration.

The conversation of happy married couples is without end, although it embrace many intervals of absence and interruption.

"Come Laura, my dear, make haste," cried Miss Owen, as she approached the lime tree. "Baby has been awake these ten minutes, and he won't wait a moment longer."

"The little despot!" ejaculated Charles Thornton, as he opened a way, through the pendant foliage, for his wife's exit. Then offering his arm to the old lady, whom he loved and respected, even more than he had promised, he took a turn with her in the garden, communicating as they walked along, to her no longer withered heart, a portion of his own felicity.

Mr. Gay's fondest wishes for his daughter's happiness, and the character of his son-in-law were fully realized. Laura felt quite sure, that had he lived to witness her union with Charles Thornton, he would have rejoiced to find himself surpassed in his son-in-law, whom he would have encouraged to persevere in a wider sphere of patriotism than had been open to himself.

THE END.

1 JA 56

LONDON:
Printed by Schulze and Co., 13, Poland Street.

CHEAP EDITION OF MISS BURNEY'S DIARY.

In Seven Volumes, small 8vo, Embellished with Portraits,

Price only 3s. each, elegantly bound, either of which may be had separately,

DIARY AND LETTERS

of

MADAME D'ARBLAY,

AUTHOR OF "EVELINA," "CECILIA," &c.

INCLUDING THE PERIOD OF

HER RESIDENCE AT THE COURT OF QUEEN CHARLOTTE.

OPINIONS OF THE PRESS.

EDINBURGH REVIEW.

"Madame D'Arblay lived to be a classic. Time set on her fame, before she went hence, that seal which is seldom set except on the fame of the departed. All those whom we have been accustomed to revere as intellectual patriarchs seemed children when compared with her; for Burke had sat up all night to read her writings, and Johnson had pronounced her superior to Fielding, when Rogers was still a schoolboy, and Southey still in petticoats. Her Diary is written in her earliest and best manner; in true woman's English, clear, natural, and lively. It ought to be consulted by every person who wishes to be well acquainted with the history of our literature and our manners."

TIMES.

"Miss Burney's work ought to be placed beside Boswell's 'Life,' to which it forms an excellent supplement."

LITERARY GAZETTE.

"This publication will take its place in the libraries beside Walpole and Boswell."

MESSENGER.

"This work may be considered a kind of supplement to Boswell's Life of Johnson. It is a beautiful picture of society as it existed in manners, taste, and literature, in the reign of George the Third, drawn by a pencil as vivid and brilliant as that of any of the celebrated persons who composed the circle."

POST.

"Miss Burney's Diary, sparkling with wit, teeming with lively anecdote and delectable gossip, and full of sound and discreet views of persons and things, will be perused with interest by all classes of readers."

CHEAP EDITION OF THE LIVES OF THE QUEENS.

Now complete, in Eight Volumes, post octavo (comprising from 600 to 700 pages each), Price only 7s. 6d. per Volume, elegantly bound, either of which may be had separately, to complete sets,

LIVES OF THE QUEENS
OF ENGLAND.

BY AGNES STRICKLAND.

Dedicated by Express Permission to her Majesty.

EMBELLISHED WITH PORTRAITS OF EVERY QUEEN,
BEAUTIFULLY ENGRAVED FROM THE MOST AUTHENTIC SOURCES.

IN announcing a cheap Edition of this important and interesting work, which has been considered unique in biographical literature, the publishers again beg to direct attention to the following extract from the author's preface:—" A revised edition of the 'Lives of the Queens of England, embodying the important collections which have been brought to light since the appearance of earlier impressions, is now offered to the world, embellished with Portraits of every Queen, from authentic and properly verified sources. The series, commencing with the consort of William the Conqueror, occupies that most interesting and important period of our national chronology, from the death of the last monarch of the Anglo-Saxon line, Edward the Confessor, to the demise of the last sovereign of the royal house of Stuart, Queen Anne, and comprises therein thirty queens who have worn the crown-matrimonial, and four the regal diadem of this realm. We have related the parentage of every queen, described her education, traced the influence of family connexions and national habits on her conduct, both public and private, and given a concise outline of the domestic, as well as the general history of her times, and its effects on her character, and we have done so with singleness of heart, unbiassed by selfish interests or narrow views. Such as they were in life we have endeavoured to portray them, both in

LIVES OF THE QUEENS—*continued.*

good and ill, without regard to any other considerations than the development of the *facts*. Their sayings, their doings, their manners, their costume, will be found faithfully chronicled in this work, which also includes the most interesting of their letters. The hope that the 'Lives of the Queens of England' might be regarded as a national work, honourable to the female character, and generally useful to society, has encouraged us to the completion of the task."

OPINIONS OF THE PRESS.

FROM THE TIMES.

"These volumes have the fascination of romance united to the integrity of history. The work is written by a lady of considerable learning, indefatigable industry, and careful judgment. All these qualifications for a biographer and an historian she has brought to bear upon the subject of her volumes, and from them has resulted a narrative interesting to all, and more particularly interesting to that portion of the community to whom the more refined researches of literature afford pleasure and instruction. The whole work should be read, and no doubt will be read, by all who are anxious for information. It is a lucid arrangement of facts, derived from authentic sources, exhibiting a combination of industry, learning, judgment, and impartiality, not often met with in biographers of crowned heads."

MORNING HERALD.

"A remarkable and truly great historical work. In this series of biographies, in which the severe truth of history takes almost the wildness of romance, it is the singular merit of Miss Strickland that her research has enabled her to throw new light on many doubtful passages, to bring forth fresh facts, and to render every portion of our annals which she has described an interesting and valuable study. She has given a most valuable contribution to the history of England, and we have no hesitation in affirming that no one can be said to possess an accurate knowledge of the history of the country who has not studied this truly national work, which, in this new edition, has received all the aids that further research on the part of the author, and of embellishment on the part of the publishers, could tend to make it still more valuable, and still more attractive, than it had been in its original form."

MORNING POST.

"We must pronounce Miss Strickland beyond all comparison the most entertaining historian in the English language. She is certainly a woman of powerful and active mind, as well as of scrupulous justice and honesty of purpose."

QUARTERLY REVIEW.

"Miss Strickland has made a very judicious use of many authentic MS. authorities not previously collected, and the result is a most interesting addition to our biographical library."

ATHENÆUM.

"A valuable contribution to historical knowledge. It contains a mass of every kind of historical matter of interest, which industry and research could collect. We have derived much entertainment and instruction from the work."

CHEAP EDITION OF PEPYS' DIARY.

Now ready, a New and Cheap Edition, printed uniformly with the last edition of EVELYN'S DIARY, *and comprising all the recent Notes and Emendations, Indexes, &c., in Four Volumes, post octavo, with Portraits, price 6s. per Volume, handsomely bound, of the*

DIARY AND CORRESPONDENCE OF

SAMUEL PEPYS, F.R.S.,

SECRETARY TO THE ADMIRALTY IN THE REIGNS OF CHARLES II. AND JAMES II.

EDITED BY RICHARD LORD BRAYBROOKE.

The authority of PEPYS, as an historian and illustrator of a considerable portion of the seventeenth century, has been so fully acknowledged by every scholar and critic, that it is now scarcely necessary to remind the reader of the advantages he possessed for producing the most complete and trustworthy record of events, and the most agreeable picture of society and manners, to be found in the literature of any nation. In confidential communication with the reigning sovereigns, holding high official employment, placed at the head of the Scientific and Learned of a period remarkable for intellectual impulse, mingling in every circle, and observing everything and everybody whose characteristics were worth noting down; and possessing, moreover, an intelligence peculiarly fitted for seizing the most graphic points in whatever he attempted to delineate, PEPYS may be considered the most valuable as well as the most entertaining of our National Historians.

A New and Cheap Edition of this work, comprising all the restored passages and the additional annotations that have been called for by the vast advances in antiquarian and historical knowledge during the last twenty years, will doubtless be regarded as one of the most agreeable additions that could be made to the library of the general reader.

CRITICAL OPINIONS ON PEPYS' DIARY.

" Without making any exception in favour of any other production of ancient or modern diarists, we unhesitatingly characterise this journal as the most remarkable production of its kind which has ever been given to the world. Pepys' Diary makes us comprehend the great historical events of the age, and the people who bore a part in them, and gives us more clear glimpses into the true English life of the times than all the other memorials of them that have come down to our own."
—*Edinburgh Review.*

"There is much in Pepys' Diary that throws a distinct and vivid light over the picture of England and its government during the period succeeding the Restoration. If, quitting the broad path of history, we look for minute information concerning ancient manners and customs, the progress of arts and sciences, and the various branches of antiquity, we have never seen a mine so rich as these volumes. The variety of Pepys' tastes and pursuits led him into almost every department of life. He was a man of business, a man of information, a man of whim, and, to a certain degree, a man of pleasure. He was a statesman, a *bel-esprit*, a virtuoso, and a connoisseur. His curiosity made him an unwearied, as well as an universal, learner, and whatever he saw found its way into his tablets."—*Quarterly Review.*

"The best book of its kind in the English language. The new matter is extremely curious, and occasionally far more characteristic and entertaining than the old. The writer is seen in a clearer light, and the reader is taken into his inmost soul. Pepys' Diary is the ablest picture of the age in which the writer lived, and a work of standard importance in English literature."—*Athenæum.*

"We place a high value on Pepys' Diary as the richest and most delightful contribution ever made to the history of English life and manners in the latter half of the seventeenth century."—*Examiner.*

"We owe Pepys a debt of gratitude for the rare and curious information he has bequeathed to us in this most amusing and interesting work. His Diary is valuable, as depicting to us many of the most important characters of the times. Its author has bequeathed to us the records of his heart—the very reflection of his energetic mind; and his quaint but happy narrative clears up numerous disputed points—throws light into many of the dark corners of history, and lays bare the hidden substratum of events which gave birth to, and supported the visible progress of, the nation."—*Tait's Magazine.*

"Of all the records that have ever been published, Pepys' Diary gives us the most vivid and trustworthy picture of the times, and the clearest view of the state of English public affairs and of English society during the reign of Charles II. We see there, as in a map, the vices of the monarch, the intrigues of the Cabinet, the wanton follies of the court, and the many calamities to which the nation was subjected during the memorable period of fire, plague, and general licentiousness."
—*Morning Post.*

Now in course of Publication,

HISTORY OF THE LANDED GENTRY,

A Genealogical Dictionary

OF THE WHOLE OF THE UNTITLED ARISTOCRACY OF ENGLAND, SCOTLAND, AND IRELAND.

ComprisingParticulars of 100,000 Individuals connected with them.

By SIR BERNARD BURKE.

Ulster King of Arms.

A new and thoroughly-revised Edition, to be completed in a single volume, uniform with the Peerage and Baronetage (divided into four parts, the first of which is now ready, price 10s. 6d.).

N.B.—Communications and Corrections intended for this Work are requested to be addressed as soon as possible to Sir B. Burke, care of the publishers, 13, Great Marlborough Street, London.

THE Landed Gentry of England are so closely connected with the stirring records of its eventful history, that some acquaintance with them is a matter of necessity with the legislator, the lawyer, the historical student, the speculator in politics, and the curious in topographical and antiquarian lore; and even the very spirit of ordinary curiosity will prompt to a desire to trace the origin and progress of those families whose influence pervades the towns and villages of our land. This work furnishes such a mass of authentic information, in regard to all the principal families in the kingdom, as has never before been attempted to be brought together. It relates to the untitled families of rank, as the "Peerage and Baronetage" does to the titled, and forms, in fact, a peerage of the untitled aristocracy. It embraces the whole of the landed interest, and is indispensable to the library of every gentleman.

"A work of this kind is of a national value. Its utility is not merely temporary, but it will exist and be acknowledged as long as the families whose names and genealogies are recorded in it continue to form an integral portion of the English constitution. As a correct record of descent, no family should be without it. The untitled aristocracy have in this great work as perfect a dictionary of their genealogical history, family connexions, and heraldic rights, as the peerage and baronetage. It will be an enduring and trustworthy record."—*Morning Post.*

"A work in which every gentleman will find a domestic interest, as it contains the fullest account of every known family in the United Kingdom. It is a dictionary of all names, families, and their origin,—of every man's neighbour and friend, if not of his own relatives and immediate connexions. It cannot fail to be of the greatest utility to professional men in their researches respecting the members of different families, heirs to property, &c. Indeed, it will become as necessary as a Directory in every office."—*Bell's Messenger.*

THE PEERAGE AND BARONETAGE
OF THE BRITISH EMPIRE.

BY SIR BERNARD BURKE,
ULSTER KING OF ARMS.

NEW EDITION, REVISED AND CORRECTED FROM THE PERSONAL COMMUNICATIONS OF THE NOBILITY, &c.

With 1500 Engravings of ARMS. In 1 vol. (comprising as much matter as twenty ordinary volumes), 38s. bound.

The following is a List of the Principal Contents of this Standard Work:—

I. A full and interesting history of each order of the English Nobility, showing its origin, rise, titles, immunities, privileges, &c.

II. A complete Memoir of the Queen and Royal Family, forming a brief genealogical History of the Sovereign of this country, and deducing the descent of the Plantagenets, Tudors, Stuarts, and Guelphs, through their various ramifications. To this section is appended a list of those Peers and others who inherit the distinguished honour of Quartering the Royal Arms of Plantagenet.

III. An Authentic table of Precedence.

IV. A perfect HISTORY OF ALL THE PEERS AND BARONETS, with the fullest details of their ancestors and descendants, and particulars respecting every collateral member of each family, and all intermarriages, &c.

V. The Spiritual Lords.

VI. Foreign Noblemen, subjects by birth of the British Crown.

VII. Extinct Peerages, of which descendants still exist.

VIII. Peerages claimed.

IX. Surnames of Peers and Peeresses, with Heirs Apparent and Presumptive.

X. Courtesy titles of Eldest Sons.

XI. Peerages of the Three Kingdoms in order of Precedence.

XII. Baronets in order of Precedence.

XIII. Privy Councillors of England and Ireland.

XIV. Daughters of Peers married to Commoners.

XV. ALL THE ORDERS OF KNIGHT-HOOD, with every Knight and all the Knights Bachelors.

XVI. Mottoes translated, with poetical illustrations.

"The most complete, the most convenient, and the cheapest work of the kind ever given to the public."—*Sun.*

"The best genealogical and heraldic dictionary of the Peerage and Baronetage, and the first authority on all questions affecting the aristocracy."—*Globe.*

"For the amazing quantity of personal and family history, admirable arrangement of details, and accuracy of information, this genealogical and heraldic dictionary is without a rival. It is now the standard and acknowledged book of reference upon all questions touching pedigree, and direct or collateral affinity with the titled aristocracy. The lineage of each distinguished house is deduced through all the various ramifications. Every collateral branch, however remotely connected, is introduced; and the alliances are so carefully inserted, as to show, in all instances, the connexion which so intimately exists between the titled and untitled aristocracy. We have also much most entertaining historical matter, and many very curious and interesting family traditions. The work is, in fact, a complete cyclopædia of the whole titled classes of the empire, supplying all the information that can possibly be desired on the subject."—*Morning Post.*

CHEAP EDITION OF THE
DIARY AND CORRESPONDENCE OF
JOHN EVELYN, F.R.S.

COMPRISING ALL THE IMPORTANT ADDITIONAL NOTES, LETTERS, AND OTHER ILLUSTRATIONS LAST MADE.

Now completed, with Portraits, in Four Volumes, post octavo (either of which may be had separately), price 6s. each, handsomely bound,

"We rejoice to welcome this beautiful and compact edition of Evelyn. It is intended as a companion to the recent edition of Pepys, and presents similar claims to interest and notice. Evelyn was greatly above the vast majority of his contemporaries, and the Diary which records the incidents in his long life, extending over the greater part of a century, is deservedly esteemed one of the most valuable and interesting books in the language. Evelyn took part in the breaking out of the civil war against Charles I., and he lived to see William of Orange ascend the throne. Through the days of Strafford and Laud, to those of Sancroft and Ken, he was the steady friend of moderation and peace in the English Church. He interceded alike for the royalist and the regicide; he was the correspondent of Cowley, the patron of Jeremy Taylor, the associate and fellow-student of Boyle; and over all the interval between Vandyck and Kneller, between the youth of Milton and the old age of Dryden, poetry and the arts found him an intelligent adviser, and a cordial friend. There are, on the whole, very few men of whom England has more reason to be proud. We heartily commend so good an edition of this English classic."—*Examiner.*

"This work is a necessary companion to the popular histories of our country, to Hume, Hallam, Macaulay, and Lingard.—*Sun.*

LIVES OF THE PRINCESSES OF ENGLAND.
By MRS. EVERETT GREEN,

In 6 vols., post 8vo, with Illustrations, 10s. 6d. each, bound.
Either of which may be had separately.

"This work is a worthy companion to Miss Strickland's admirable 'Queens of England.' That celebrated work, although its heroines were, for the most part, foreign Princesses, related almost entirely to the history of this country. The Princesses of England, on the contrary, are themselves English, but their lives are nearly all connected with foreign nations. Their biographies, consequently, afford us a glimpse of the manners and customs of the chief European kingdoms, a circumstance which not only gives to the work the charm of variety, but which is likely to render it peculiarly useful to the general reader, as it links together by association the contemporaneous history of various nations. We cordially commend Mrs. Green's production to general attention; it is (necessarily) as useful as history, and fully as entertaining as romance."—*Sun.*

SIR B. BURKE'S DICTIONARY OF THE
EXTINCT, DORMANT, AND ABEYANT PEERAGES
OF ENGLAND, SCOTLAND AND IRELAND.

Beautifully printed, in 1 vol. 8vo, containing 800 double-column pages,
21s. bound.

This work connects, in many instances, the new with the old nobility, and it
will in all cases show the cause which has influenced the revival of an extinct
dignity in a new creation. It should be particularly noticed, that this new work
appertains nearly as much to extant as to extinct persons of distinction; for
though dignities pass away, it rarely occurs that whole families do.

THE ROMANCE OF THE ARISTOCRACY;
OR,
ANECDOTICAL RECORDS OF DISTINGUISHED FAMILIES.
By SIR BERNARD BURKE.

NEW AND CHEAPER EDITION, 3 vols., post 8vo.

" The most curious incidents, the most stirring tales, and the most remarkable
circumstances connected with the histories, public and private, of our noble houses
and aristocratic families, are here given in a shape which will preserve them
in the library, and render them the favourite study of those who are interested
in the romance of real life. These stories, with all the reality of established fact,
read with as much spirit as the tales of Boccaccio, and are as full of strange
matter for reflection and amazement."—*Britannia*.

SKETCHES OF THE IRISH BAR;
INCLUDING
A JOURNAL OF CONVERSATIONS WITH CHIEF-JUSTICE
BUSHE, NOW FIRST PUBLISHED;

WITH OTHER LITERARY AND POLITICAL ESSAYS.
By WILLIAM HENRY CURRAN, Esq.

2 vols. post 8vo, 21s. bound.

" Mr. Curran's sketches have many claims on our attention. The conversations with Chief-Justice Bushe—a charming collection of curious anecdotes—are
full of interest, and are now printed for the first time. Mr. Curran's own recollections of celebrated persons are just as striking as those of Chief-Justice
Bushe."—*Athenæum*.

" These papers will be welcomed anew for their animated style, their graphic
and sometimes romantic narratives, for the pictures they give of many famous
men now passed away, and for the conscientious accuracy and perfect good taste
which has governed the writing of them."—*Examiner*.

REVELATIONS OF PRINCE TALLEYRAND.

Second Edition, 1 volume, post 8vo, with Portrait, 10s. 6d. bound.

"We have perused this work with extreme interest. It is a portrait of Talleyrand drawn by his own hand."—*Morning Post.*

"A more interesting work has not issued from the press for many years. It is in truth a most complete Boswell sketch of the greatest diplomatist of the age."—*Sunday Times.*

THE LIFE AND REIGN OF CHARLES I.
By I. DISRAELI.

A NEW EDITION. REVISED BY THE AUTHOR, AND EDITED BY HIS SON, THE RT. HON. B. DISRAELI, M.P. 2 vols., 8vo, 28s. bound.

"By far the most important work on the important age of Charles I. that modern times have produced."—*Quarterly Review.*

MEMOIRS OF SCIPIO DE RICCI,
LATE BISHOP OF PISTOIA AND PRATO;
REFORMER OF CATHOLICISM IN TUSCANY.

Cheaper Edition, 2 vols. 8vo, 12s. bound.

The leading feature of this important work is its application to the great question now at issue between our Protestant and Catholic fellow-subjects. It contains a complete *exposé* of the Romish Church Establishment during the eighteenth century, and of the abuses of the Jesuits throughout the greater part of Europe. Many particulars of the most thrilling kind are brought to light.

HISTORIC SCENES.
By AGNES STRICKLAND.

Author of "Lives of the Queens of England," &c. 1 vol., post 8vo, elegantly bound, with Portrait of the Author, 10s. 6d.

"This attractive volume is replete with interest. Like Miss Strickland's former works, it will be found, we doubt not, in the hands of youthful branches of a family as well as in those of their parents, to all and each of whom it cannot fail to be alike amusing and instructive."—*Britannia.*

MEMOIRS OF PRINCE ALBERT;
AND THE HOUSE OF SAXONY.

Second Edition, revised, with Additions, by Authority.
1 vol., post 8vo, with Portrait, bound, 6s.

MADAME CAMPAN'S MEMOIRS
OF THE COURT OF MARIE ANTOINETTE.

Cheaper Edition, 2 vols. 8vo, with Portraits, price 7s.

"We have seldom perused so entertaining a work. It is as a mirror of the most splendid Court in Europe, at a time when the monarchy had not been shorn of any of its beams, that it is particularly worthy of attention."—*Chronicle.*

LIFE AND LETTERS OF THE EMPRESS JOSEPHINE.

3 vols., small 8vo, 15s.

"A curious and entertaining piece of domestic biography of a most extraordinary person, under circumstances almost unprecedented."—*New Monthly.*
"An extremely amusing book, full of anecdotes and traits of character of kings, princes, nobles, generals," &c.—*Morning Journal.*

MEMOIRS OF A HUNGARIAN LADY.
MADAME PULSZKY.

WRITTEN BY HERSELF. 2 vols., 12s. bound.

"Worthy of a place by the side of the Memoirs of Madame de Staël and Madame Campan."—*Globe.*

MEMOIRS AND CORRESPONDENCE OF
SIR ROBERT MURRAY KEITH, K.B.,

Minister Plenipotentiary at the Courts of Dresden, Copenhagen, and Vienna, from 1769 to 1793; with Biographical Memoirs of

QUEEN CAROLINE MATILDA, SISTER OF GEORGE III.

Cheaper Edition. Two vols., post 8vo, with Portraits, 15s. bound.

Now ready, PART XI., price 5s., of

M. A. THIERS' HISTORY OF FRANCE
UNDER NAPOLEON.

A SEQUEL TO HIS HISTORY OF THE FRENCH REVOLUTION.

As guardian to the archives of the state, M. Thiers had access to diplomatic papers and other documents of the highest importance, hitherto known only to a privileged few. From private sources M. Thiers has also derived much valuable information. Many interesting memoirs, diaries, and letters, all hitherto unpublished, and most of them destined for political reasons to remain so, have been placed at his disposal; while all the leading characters of the empire, who were alive when the author undertook the present history, have supplied him with a mass of incidents and anecdotes which have never before appeared in print.

N.B. Any of the Parts may, for the present, be had separately, at 5s. each.

THE QUEENS
BEFORE THE CONQUEST.
BY MRS. MATTHEW HALL.

2 vols. post 8vo, embellished with Portraits, price 21s. bound.

"Mrs. Hall's work presents a clear and connected series of records of the early female sovereigns of England, of whom only a few scattered anecdotes have hitherto been familiarly known to general readers. The book is of great interest, as containing many notices of English life and manners in the remote times of our British, Roman, Saxon, and Danish ancestors."—*Literary Gazette.*

"These volumes open up a new and interesting page of history to the majority of readers. What Miss Strickland has achieved for English Queens since the Norman era, has been accomplished by Mrs. Hall on behalf of the royal ladies who, as wives of Saxon kings, have influenced the destinies of Britain."—*Sunday Times.*

"Mrs. Hall may be congratulated on having successfully accomplished a very arduous undertaking. Her volumes form a useful introduction to the usual commencement of English history."—*Sun.*

"These interesting volumes have been compiled with judgment, discretion, and taste. Mrs. Hall has spared neither pains nor labour to make her history worthy of the characters she has essayed to illustrate. The book is, in every sense, an addition of decided value to the annals of the British people."—*Bell's Messenger*

"Of all our female historico-biographical writers, Mrs. Hall seems to us to be one of the most painstaking, erudite, and variously and profoundly accomplished. Her valuable volumes contain not only the lives of the Queens before the Conquest, but a very excellent history of England previously to the Norman dynasty."—*Observer.*

THE CRESCENT AND THE CROSS;
OR, ROMANCE AND REALITIES OF EASTERN TRAVEL.
By ELIOT WARBURTON.

TWELFTH EDITION, in 1 vol., with 15 Illustrations, 6s. bound.

"A book calculated to prove more practically useful was never penned than the 'Crescent and the Cross'—a work which surpasses all others in its homage for the sublime and its love for the beautiful in those famous regions consecrated to everlasting immortality in the annals of the prophets—and which no other modern writer has ever depicted with a pencil at once so reverent and so picturesque."—*Sun.*

LORD LINDSAY'S LETTERS ON THE HOLY LAND.

FOURTH EDITION, Revised, 1 vol., post 8vo, with Illustrations, 6s. bound.

"Lord Lindsay has felt and recorded what he saw with the wisdom of a philosopher, and the faith of an enlightened Christian."—*Quarterly Review.*

NARRATIVE OF A
TWO YEARS' RESIDENCE AT NINEVEH;
With Remarks on the Chaldeans, Nestorians, Yezidees, &c.
By the Rev. J. P. FLETCHER.

Cheaper Edition. Two vols., post 8vo, 12s. bound.

ADVENTURES IN GEORGIA, CIRCASSIA, AND RUSSIA.
By Lieutenant-Colonel G. POULETT CAMERON, C.B., K.T.S., &c.

2 vols., post 8vo, bound, 12s.

CAPTAINS KING AND FITZROY.
NARRATIVE OF THE TEN YEARS' VOYAGE ROUND THE WORLD,
OF H.M.S. ADVENTURE AND BEAGLE.

Cheaper Edition, in 2 large vols. 8vo, with Maps, Charts, and upwards of Sixty Illustrations, by Landseer, and other eminents Artists, price 1l. 11s. 6d. bound.

"One of the most interesting narratives of voyaging that it has fallen to our lot to notice, and which must always occupy a distinguished space in the history of scientific navigation."—*Quarterly Review.*

JAPAN AND THE JAPANESE,

Comprising the Narrative of a Three Years' Residence in Japan, with an Account of British Commercial Intercourse with that Country.

By CAPTAIN GOLOWNIN.

NEW and CHEAPER EDITION. 2 vols. post 8vo, 10s. bound.

"No European has been able, from personal observation and experience, to communicate a tenth part of the intelligence furnished by this writer."—*British Review.*

STORY OF THE PENINSULAR WAR.

A COMPANION VOLUME TO MR. GLEIG'S

"STORY OF THE BATTLE OF WATERLOO."

With Six Portraits and Map, 5s. bound.

THE NEMESIS IN CHINA;

COMPRISING A COMPLETE

HISTORY OF THE WAR IN THAT COUNTRY.

From Notes of Captain W. H. HALL, R.N.

1 vol., Plates, 6s. bound.

"Capt. Hall's narrative of the services of the *Nemesis* is full of interest, and will, we are sure, be valuable hereafter, as affording most curious materials for the history of steam navigation."—*Quarterly Review.*

CAPTAIN CRAWFORD'S NAVAL REMINISCENCES;

COMPRISING MEMOIRS OF

ADMIRALS SIR E. OWEN, SIR B. HALLOWELL CAREW, AND OTHER DISTINGUISHED COMMANDERS.

2 vols., post 8vo, with Portraits, 12s. bound.

ADVENTURES OF A SOLDIER.

WRITTEN BY HIMSELF.

Being the Memoirs of EDWARD COSTELLO, of the Rifle Brigade, and late Captain in the British Legion. Cheap Edition, with Portrait, 3s. 6d. bound.

"An excellent book of its class. A true and vivid picture of a soldier's life."—*Athenæum.*

"This highly interesting volume is filled with details and anecdotes of the most startling character, and well deserves a place in the library of every regiment in the service."—*Naval and Military Gazette.*

SALATHIEL, THE IMMORTAL.

By the Rev. GEORGE CROLY, LL.D.

New Revised and Cheaper Edition, in 1 vol. post 8vo, 10s. 6d.

" A magnificent fiction. One of the most splendid productions among works of fiction that the age has brought forth."—*Athenæum.*

" This extraordinary story, the production of a man of great genius, cannot be classed with any of the works of imagination which have been put forth in these times, so fertile in romance. It is perfectly original in the general conception, as well as in its splendid and powerful eloquence."—*Literary Gazette.*

" This is a work of very peculiar character. It is, in fact, the autobiography of the Wandering Jew, and contains a history of the troubles, insurrections, persecutions, &c., which supervened in Judea, immediately after the death of Christ. Dr. Croly has well succeeded in depicting the Jewish character and warfare; and has entered with considerable felicity into what it is probable would be the feelings of such a being as the impious and miserable wanderer whose history he writes."—*Weekly Review.*

Cheaper Edition, in 3 vols., price 10s. 6d., half-bound,

FORTUNE: A STORY OF LONDON LIFE.

By D. T. COULTON, Esq.

" A brilliant novel. A more vivid picture of various phases of society has not been painted since ' Vivian Grey' first dazzled and confounded the world; but it is the biting satire of fashionable life, the moral anatomy of high society, which will attract all readers. In every sense of the word, ' Fortune' is an excellent novel."—*Observer.*

THE MODERN ORLANDO.

By Dr. CROLY.

1 vol. post 8vo, 5s.

"By far the best thing of the kind that has been written since Byron."— *Literary Gazette.*

THE HALL AND THE HAMLET.

By WILLIAM HOWITT.

Author of " The Book of the Seasons," " Rural Life in England," &c.
Cheaper Edition, 2 vols., post 8vo, 12s. bound.

HURST AND BLACKETT, PUBLISHERS,

SUCCESSORS TO HENRY COLBURN,

13, GREAT MARLBOROUGH STREET.

CPSIA information can be obtained at www.ICGtesting.com
Printed in the USA
BVOW05s1226061015

421173BV00017B/294/P

9 781241 191221